Doing Good or Doing Well?

Japan's Foreign Aid Program

MARGEE M. ENSIGN

Doing Good
or Doing Well?

Japan's Foreign Aid Program

WITHDRAWN

Columbia University Press   NEW YORK

Columbia University Press
New York   Oxford
Copyright © 1992 Columbia University Press
All rights reserved

Library of Congress Cataloging-in-Publication Data

Ensign, Margee M., 1954–
    Doing good or doing well? : Japan's foreign aid program / Margee
Ensign.
        p.   cm.
    Includes bibliographical references and index.
    ISBN 0-231-08144-8
    1. Economic assistance, Japanese.   I. Title.
    HC60.E473   1992
    338.9′152—dc20   92-31536
                                                                        CIP

Designer: Jennifer Dossin

Printed in the United States of America

c 10 9 8 7 6 5 4 3 2 1

To my parents and Katherine,
For love, wisdom and inspiration

CONTENTS

Warm Hopes, Cold Numbers

Japan's emergence as a world economic power is second only to the end of the Cold War in its significance for the world's political economy. While volumes have already been written profiling Japan's behavior in trade and finance, less has been written about a third facet of its economic personality—its foreign aid program.

Since there had not previously been much hard data on that subject, when Japan's Ministry of Foreign Affairs released foreign aid figures in 1990, they received wide attention, especially since they indicated that Japanese aid policy was taking a new direction. The figures effectively documented that the percentage of foreign firms winning contracts for Japanese aid projects financed through loans had increased dramatically since 1986. Japan appeared to be undergoing a fundamental shift away from support for its commercial interests (through aid tied to exports) to one more open to international competition.

The statistics were widely embraced by scholars and policymakers alike. The Tokyo Declaration on the U.S. Japan Global Partnership signed in January 1992 by President Bush and Prime Minister Miyazawa even cited the data in its text:

"More than eighty percent [of Japan's official development assistance in loans] have already been untied. The procurement of American firms accounted for 5 percent or 37 billion yen, of Japan's ODA loans in FY 1990.[1]"

Certainly, all foreign assistance is motivated by the specific interests of the donor, whether they are of a political, security, economic, or humanitarian nature. One viewpoint holds that Japan's foreign aid program, despite these statistics, remains more commercially oriented than most and that official development assistance (ODA) is used to further Japan's narrow economic interests. But most analysts have accepted these and other aggregate statistics Japan has submitted to the Development Assistance Committee (DAC)—the donor coordination component of the Organization for Economic Development (OECD)—that indicate Japan's aid is among the least tied of any donor's. They have concluded that while Japanese assistance is more regionally biased toward its economic partners, it is still not "tied" in any meaningful way to Japanese commercial interests.

The difficulty of collecting primary data on procurement has discouraged the kind of empirical research that might substantiate or refute such viewpoints.

This author had also accepted the data on untying and embarked in 1990 on a project to do case studies of American firms reported to have won the aid contracts: the five percent cited in the Tokyo Declaration. Only five American firms could be identified, despite extensive searches, with assistance from Japan's loan agency, the Overseas Economic Cooperation Fund (OECF), Japan's International Cooperation Agency (JICA) and the Embassy of Japan in Washington, D.C. In 1991, OECF, JICA and the Embassy released the names of non-Japanese companies that had won bids on OECF-financed loan projects. The data released from OECF listed no American companies. The companies named by the Embassy were all American companies, but follow-up with the companies themselves revealed that they had either not bid on such projects or had bid and lost.

In the arena of Japanese bilateral foreign aid loans, then, only five American firms have actually secured a contract and in general very few non-Japanese firms have won yen loan-financed aid contracts. The data presented in this study, then, on Japanese bilateral foreign aid loans, support a contrary view: that Japan's foreign aid program is still very tied to Japanese business interests. A detailed report on this search and its outcome is presented in chapter 3.

These findings forced this author to reexamine her theoretical orientation and some conventional wisdoms about this topic. Unfortunately there has been no shortage of opinion, debate, or assertions about Japan's aid—only a shortage of data. Teaching three semesters of graduate students about "Quantitative Approaches to International Politics" in the course of this research, however, provided good counsel. A thesis of that course is that paradigms or theoretical assumptions can guide research to the degree that data-driven conclusions that would contradict a dominant theory are in danger of being ignored.

The research presented in this study came close to being ignored. Several U.S. colleagues suggested not publishing the findings, as they could jeopardize an already tenuous relationship with the Japanese. In this author's opinion, the only responsible position available to any scholar is continued research.

Much more empirical work is needed to chart a productive path in foreign aid. The results of this study, if nothing more, reveal the importance of informing national policy with sound studies.

A long-term perspective is even more critical today than in the past. Japan has become one of the world's largest donors of official development assistance, while the United States is entering a new era with its allies of shared responsibilities.

Aid postures struck now could have a long-term and irreversible impact on global welfare—not the least of which would be on the environment. Information about the disastrous effects of some narrowly based capital projects is starting to accumulate, for example. Meanwhile, the kind of investment in human resources, such as education, which has laid the foundation for Japan and the United States' own prosperity, is on the wane.

By now it should be clear to a new generation that choices made in global development to address poverty, growth, and environmental degradation are critical to our own welfare. More than 20 percent of the world's people are diseased, in poor health, or malnourished.

Yet competition with Japan and its impact on our domestic economy have created enormous political pressure in the U.S. for retrenchment to a tied aid policy, and its corresponding preference for infrastructure, before we fully understand what that concentration may bring about.

For its part, Japan today is not offering the long-range vision in foreign aid that is required of a major world leader and economic superpower. Yet Japanese foreign assistance programs may be the only ones to grow in the 1990s. It will be critical to understand their workings and to cultivate their potential for "doing good." To this end, the author offers her research and her recommendations for improving the Japanese model.

ACKNOWLEDGMENTS

Many people helped to shape this book and forced me to clarify and reexamine certain arguments, including, Peter de Leon, Larry Nowels, Katharine Knutsen, Robert L. Lurensky, Richard Forrest, and Renee Marlin-Bennett. Midway through the research, Lori Forman, and Robert M. Orr, Jr. made useful suggestions and comments. Throughout the undertaking, Stephen D. Cohen at The American University provided wisdom and insight into the overall relationship between the United States and Japan. I am also grateful for the comments and criticisms of several anonymous reviewers. Any interpretation of these comments are, of course, the author's responsibility.

My colleagues at the Development Studies Program—Mike Rock, Peter Askin, Ken Kusterer and Sam Samarasinghe—provided both good counsel and good humor during this process. William Bertrand of Tulane University deserves a special thanks for his insight and support.

I was extremely fortunate to have three excellent research assistants, Sharon Van Pelt, Raymond Gonzales, and Elena Shirley, while writing the manuscript. My thanks for their hard work and enthusiasm.

I am especially grateful to those who helped in the preparation of the manuscript: Alan Aronson provided both editorial and computer support, Sue Bernstein made extremely useful and creative editorial comments, and Steven Hansch produced the graphs. Roger LeGere deserves thanks for his constant encouragement. Special appreciation goes to Kate Wittenberg, Editor-in-Chief of Columbia University Press, for her interest and encouragement, and manuscript editor Leslie Bialler for his suggestions.

My family has played an important part in my work. My thanks to my parents and niece, Deborah Lantz, who spent many hours with my daughter so that I could finish this manuscript, and to my sisters, Janie Hofmeister for her support and Judith Lantz for a quiet place to work.

Doing Good or Doing Well?
Japan's Foreign Aid Program

There are no longer any grounds for claiming that Japanese aid is driven by the promotion of exports or commercialism.

Ministry of Foreign Affairs,
Japan's Official Development Assistance,
1990 Annual Report.

1

Toward an Empirical Approach to High-Stakes Questions

BACKGROUND

In 1989 Japan surpassed the United States as the world's largest foreign assistance donor. Japanese official development assistance or ODA rose from $1.14 billion in 1975 to $3.3 billion in 1980. By 1989, net disbursements reached $8.9 billion. In real terms from 1980 to 1988, Japanese ODA grew 41 percent. While statistics for 1990 indicate that the United State regained the top aid position, it is nevertheless clear that Japan today is one of the world's foreign aid leaders.

Japan now contributes 16.8 percent of all assistance from the member countries of the Development Assistance Committee or DAC (see table 1.1 and figure 1.1). Moreover, the decline in the 1980s of the assistance budgets of many major donors has made Japan an increasingly important

Table 1.1. Japanese Official Development Assistance
1975–90 (net disbursements)

	1975	1980	1985	1988	1989	1990*
Volume ($ mil)	$1,148	$3,353	$3,797	$9,134	$8,965	$9,069
% of GNP	.23%	.32%	.29%	.32%	.31%	.31%
% of Total DAC	8.50%	12.28%	12.90%	18.99%	19.20%	16.81%

* Preliminary
Source: OECD, *Development Cooperation*, Various years.

presence in the economies of many developing countries. As Japan's 1990 *Official Development Assistance Report* shows, Japan is now the largest donor in 26 developing countries (see appendix 1.1). In December 1991, the Japanese government announced its plan to increase overseas development assistance by 7.8 percent in fiscal 1992.

As the political rationale for many older aid programs in the Third World collapses with the end of the Cold War, Japan's more economically motivated assistance may be one of the few donor programs that continues to grow during the 1990s. Such preeminence for Japanese aid requires students of development assistance to take careful and accurate measure of its dimensions.

What are the implications of Japan's rise to preeminence in the foreign aid area? While Japan's assistance poses the possibility of new models and new outcomes, there have been too many experts on all sides of the debate speaking without data in a sincere attempt to answer the following questions:

■ What drives Japanese foreign assistance? Is this an example of a mercantilist strategy to develop and control markets and/or a reflection of Japan's desire for

international acceptance and prestige, through "burden-sharing"?

■ What is the impact of Japanese ODA on the less developed countries (LDCs) who are the recipients of Japanese economic assistance?

■ What does Japan's new status as a leader in foreign
aid mean for the United States and for the world
economy?

These are important questions to answer, but they must be
pursued with sound data. This book offers an empirical
study based on procurement statistics and its findings contradict official statistics showing Japan's aid program moving away from a commercial orientation. It is the author's
belief that the data presented here should be used to inform
our understanding of what drives and influences Japanese
foreign assistance.

The motivations of a foreign aid program, translated into
specific policies and projects, may sharply affect the outcome of foreign assistance in recipient nations. Moreover,
the perception of Japan's motivations and goals in foreign
aid will be a key factor in whether United States and Japanese aid policy can evolve cooperatively.

The United States and Japan are the world's two major
economic superpowers; together they account for one-third
of the world's yearly production of goods and services. As
competition and hostility threaten the relationship between the U.S. and Japan, some see development assistance
as the last frontier for cooperation. In Julia Chang Bloch's
words, "the area of development assistance still offers the
hope for collaboration rather than conflict."[1]

Finally, understanding what drives Japanese aid may also
give us some clues about the type of leadership role Japan
is prepared to undertake in the international economic arena
overall.

Figure 1.1. Japanese Official Development Assistance

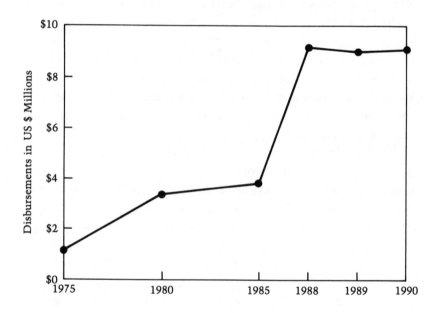

Source: OECD, *Development Cooperation*, Various Years

A LITERATURE REVIEW

Most explanations of Japanese state behavior have so far been based on knowledge of Japanese actions and policies in trade and finance, without looking at foreign aid.

Conversely, assumptions about Japan's new role in foreign aid are often informed by opinions of Japan's goals and objectives in the international economic and political system. These theoretical perspectives are sharply divided and firmly held. Karel van Wolferen depicts Japanese behavior in active, mercantilist terms: "Japanese political and economic behavior is meant to accomplish aims that are fundamentally different from those assumed by the United States ... Japanese manufacturers and financial institutions that operate internationally, and the domestic industries and industrial federations tied to them, indicate what they consider to be their international task by striving for ever greater global market shares."[2]

Ronald Morse supports this view of Japan's behavior based on social patterns—personal and institutional relationships—that resemble a cobweb: "concentric circles linked by crosscutting ties, all with a central focus."[3] Morse's central focus is a Japan striving for economic self-sufficiency and superiority.

Ezra Vogel also describes a Japan that is forming a clear vision of its leadership role in the international political economy. "For the first time since 1853, when [Commodore] Matthew Perry forced the opening of Japan's ports to foreign trade, the Japanese feel strong enough to achieve their long cherished patriotic dream: to resist with all due politeness-foreign pressures to accept arrangements that give advantages to other countries."[4]

Richard Rosecrance and Jennifer Taw take an opposite approach. They argue that Japan, having become the world's largest creditor, has a self interest in maintaining a stable international economic system. According to them, Japan is evolving toward the role of a cooperative hegemon:

"Japan's current economic actions are not consistent with either strategy [export and domestic stimulus strategies]. Their ambivalent character is reflective not of a predatory strategy, but of an emerging orientation that considers the maintenance of the international trading and financial system to be important, along with any sectarian advantage to Japan."[5]

A middle ground perspective sees Japanese foreign economic behavior as essentially "reactive" to foreign pressure, particularly that emanating from the United States. "The reactive state interpretation," according to Calder, merely maintains that the impetus to policy change is typically supplied by outside pressure, and that reaction prevails over strategy in the relatively narrow range of cases where the two come into conflict."[6]

A much more evolutionary and historical perspective on Japanese motivations characterizes most of the literature in the foreign aid area. It depicts three major phases in the Japanese aid program:

Phase one began in the 1950s with $1.2 billion in reparations payments to Burma, the Philippines, Indonesia, and Vietnam. During the second phase, from the 1960s through the late 1970s Japanese aid was commercially motivated. Japanese assistance during this period, targeted primarily at Asian countries, was seen as an overt strategy to develop markets and ensure stable sources of raw materials. The current Japanese aid program is characterized by a number of perceived goals, including political and security interests, and the desire for prestige and acceptance in the international community.[7]

Evolutionists conclude that popular perceptions of the Japanese aid program, at least in the United States, are stuck in the second phase; a period when aid was used quite consciously to promote and underwrite trade relations. Numerous articles, both in the U.S. and Japan, refer to the "illusion" that Japan's aid program is still based on commercial interests. For example:

- "Americans continue to believe that Japan's foreign aid program is mainly used to satisfy the commercial interests of Japanese business. A few examples in which American firms were shut out from international tenderings because [only LDCs could bid on certain OECF loans], make the American side have this illusion. This belief is the main cause of irritation on the American side about both Japan's and U.S. aid systems."[8]

- "To a large degree, other donors continue to view Japan's assistance program as a thinly disguised flow of export subsidies. In many ways this view is misinformed and inconsistent. Japan has opened its program over the last ten to fifteen years, and foreign contractors are increasingly winning awards through Japan's aid program.[9]

- "We should also put the record straight about the tying of aid. The following figures [showing untied aid as a percentage of total ODA] come from the OECD: [For Japan, the 1984–85 average was 69.5; for 1985–1986 it was 69.7; for the United States, the figures were 46.6 and 50.6; the total DAC was 54.9.]

- "The statistics hardly support the Joint Economic Committee's of the U.S. Congress adverse comment on Japan's tying 'reputation.' "[10]

While the Japanese aid program can still be criticized in a number of important areas—lack of globalization, slow progress on quality, the focus on capital projects—on the whole, Japan is, according to this perspective, playing a role that the U.S. can no longer afford. This role benefits both the U.S. and the recipients in the developing country.

Explanations of Japan's behavior in the aid area frequently cite domestic politics rather than an international strategy. Aid policy is considered less coherent and more malleable than trade policy. Moreover, no overarching philosophy is attributed to the aid program. This lack is thought to be due, mainly, to the bureaucratic structure underlying the formulation of aid policy.

Rix points out the importance of bureaucratic politics in shaping and hindering the development of aid policy: "divided political and bureaucratic responsibility for foreign aid has led to fragmented budget processes and a lack of any overall aid planning. . . . there is a dislocation between the political and administrative structures for aid. The importance of aid policy at the budgetary and implementation levels, and in the international arena, is not reflected in domestic structures.[11]

Orr, in a comprehensive survey of foreign aid policy-making, builds on Rix's study but, like Calder, points to the importance of external actors in influencing policy-making. Transnational relations, according to Orr, affect both bureaucratic politics and policy-making.

While recognizing the importance of bureaucratic hauling and tugging among the four major actors involved in foreign aid policy-making—the Ministry of Foreign Affairs (MOFA), the Ministry of Finance (MOF), the Ministry of International Trade and Industry (MITI) and the Economic Planning Agency (EPA)—Orr documents the importance of the U.S. as an external actor able to influence Japanese aid policy-making at critical junctures in the relationship.

His analysis indicates that neither the bureaucratic politics nor the transnational relations perspectives alone are sufficient to explain policy-making in the aid area. Instead a model that takes this external influence into account, what Orr calls a "preemptive" response, is more accurate:

we can define preemptive as delivering of a benefit to a government which may be about to affect the interests of the deliverer in a negative manner. The benefit delivered may be an inconsequential cost to the delivering nation both materially and in terms of bureaucratic dynamics. It might also include a perception by the benefit-delivering nations that some undefinable benefits may be received in return. The case of foreign aid is highly representative of preemptive transgovernmental politics. When Japan proffers an aid package at a critical period in U.S.–Japan trade relations, this is often an action that is perhaps easier for Tokyo to undertake than it would be, for example, to make concessions on a contentious trade issue.[12]

Again, Japan does not have an overall philosophical approach toward assistance. According to this view, policymaking is developed and directed both by bureaucratic concerns and frequently in reaction to international pressure, particularly that emanating from the United States.

An exception to this perspective is developed by Arase (1989). He concludes that Japanese aid policy is, and always has been, driven by an industrial policy. Japanese reparations after World War II, the concomitant bureaucratic structure (*Yon Shocho Kyogi Taisei*) and the request based system that arose during this period are used to channel monies that complement Japan's industrial policy and international economic objectives. Moreover, according to Arase, since the 1980s, a new policy has emerged from Tokyo to coordinate ODA, trade, and foreign investment and develop a regional economy in Southeast Asia. These economies are acting essentially as subcontractors to Japanese industries. Arase's conclusions are based on a pattern of aggregate trade and foreign investment statistics and a more involved stance by Japanese aid officials in LDC Ministries.

AID AND IMPLEMENTATION

What has been missing from the analysis of Japanese aid is a detailed picture of who is implementing Japanese aid projects in the field. Unlike past studies of Japanese foreign assistance, which have focused on policy-making, this study examines the implementation of Japanese foreign assistance at the private sector level.

Policy analysts have begun to surmise that the implementation phase may be the "apparent illusive missing link between policy selection and the delivered product."[13] The need to examine implementation is particularly true for Japanese aid. Its policy-making bureaucracy is highly centralized and located, for the most part, in Tokyo. Also, the rising volume of foreign assistance has not been matched by an increase in administrative staff. Both of these facts increase the potential for slippage between the making of policy and its implementation. The potential role of the private sector in implementation is greatly increased. The staff involved in administration and implementation is small compared to those of the other major donors (see table 1.2) and has not kept pace with the increase in ODA volume (see figure 1.2). There are approximately 1,500 staff members in Tokyo and overseas to oversee Japan's foreign assistance program.

Moreover, according to recent estimates, those in charge of ODA-financed loans handle approximately four times as much in funding as lending officers at the World Bank.[14] The paucity of staff involved in implementing Japan's aid program, combined with the request-based system (*Yosei Shugi*), where a developing country "requests" aid monies for a specific project, further begs the question of who actually implements Japanese foreign assistance. Japan has very recently begun to discuss moving away from the re-

Table 1.2. Aid Staff Involved with ODA: Headquarters
and Overseas

		Selected Donors and Years			
	Japan	USA	UK	West Germany	Canada
Total Number of Staff	1,490	3,552	1,633	3,684	1,264
Year	(1990)	(1989)	(1987)	(1987)	(1987)

Source: Ministry of Foreign Affairs, 1990 and Forrest (1989).

quest-based system by indicating that it will first consider a country's record on human rights and arms control but it still dominates the aid process.

Requests for assistance are clearly not one-way. A great deal of interaction occurs with Japanese consultants and survey teams who assist the developing countries in preparing their requests. Until very recently, this portion of the aid process was tied—only Japanese consultants and trading companies could assist in the preparation of requests. This fact, more than any other, led many to conclude that the aid program was de facto tied: requests were often developed such that only Japanese companies could meet the contract specifications. A project from Thailand illustrates this problem. In 1983, Thammasat University in Thailand received approval to acquire computer systems using Japanese foreign aid. After the project was approved, "problems occurred at the implementation stage, that is, with the purchasing. When the project was approved, the Japanese government in Tokyo selected the contractors. Apparently there was only one company, NEC, that won the bid because the proposal specified particular equipment that only NEC could supply."[15] One of the problems with

Figure 1.2. Relative Increase in Japan's ODA and Staff

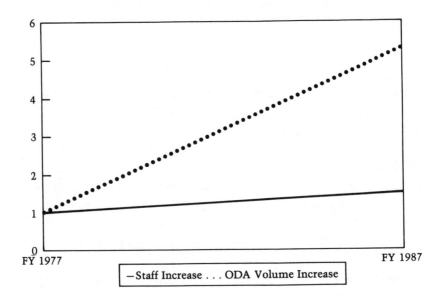

FY 1977   FY 1987

—Staff Increase . . . ODA Volume Increase

Sources: Japan's *Official Development Assistance Annual Report 1990*, Ministry of Foreign Affairs, and Forrest, 1989

the equipment was that the university needed printers that could print both English and Thai. At the time NEC did not have such printers.

Finally, the project-oriented nature of the Japanese aid program, where the bulk of assistance is in yen loans for infrastructure projects (also called capital projects assistance), further ensures a Japanese presence in the recipient country. Basic infrastructure assistance is defined as aid to areas such as telecommunications, transportation, and energy. From 1966 through 1989, an average of 52.5 percent of Japanese assistance was in these three sectors (see table 1.3 and figure 1.3).

This technology-intensive assistance requires a high level of imported capital goods and is thus potentially very lucrative to the donor's export-oriented industries. The orientation of Japan's aid program toward assistance for capital has led to the hypothesis that there is a strong aid/trade/ private sector link in this portion of the aid program, i.e., that this type of assistance supports the efforts of Japanese industries to establish and deepen export markets. An example of this is the Asahan hydroelectric project in Sumatra, Indonesia. "It was designed in part by one of Japan's largest ODA consulting firms, Nippon Koei. The OECF provided loans totaling over $100 million, two-thirds of the funding for a hydroelectric dam and associated transmission lines and roads. The low-cost electric power was then used by Asahan Aluminum, a joint venture company formed by the Indonesian government, five Japanese smelting companies, and seven *sogo-shoshas* (general trading companies)."[16]

The case illustrates key criticisms leveled at the Japanese aid program: its tying status and its sectoral orientation. An exploration of these issues can begin to help us understand and explain the motivations of the aid program.

Table 1.3. Sectoral Distribution of OECF Loans to Foreign
Governments (Commitment Basis)

Fiscal Year	Electricity, Power and Gas	Transpor- tation	Telecom- munications	Irrigation and Flood Control	Agriculture, Forestry and Fisheries
FY 1988	158.9	172.4	38.4	37.7	2.7
%	14.6	15.8	3.5	3.5	0.2
FY 1989	104.1	195.0	65.7	46.0	0.0
%	12.3	23.0	7.8	5.4	0.0
Total 66–89	1,893.0	2,101.0	566.8	429.4	169.2
%	21.8	24.2	6.5	4.9	2.0

Source: OECF *Annual Report*, 1990.

TYING STATUS

 ying status relates to the level of restrictions on the procurement of goods and services. The OECD has defined three major categories related to tying status:

- generally untied;
- partially (or LDC) untied;
- tied.

The first category, generally untied, means that aid monies can be used to purchase goods and services world-wide, that they are not "tied" to any specific country. Partially or LDC untied allows the recipient country to use aid for procurement from the donor and most other developing countries. Finally, tied aid means that procurement is to be primarily (but not necessarily totally) made from the donor country.

Statistics released by the Ministry of Foreign Affairs show that 60 percent of Japanese aid in 1974 was tied to procurements from Japan. In 1978, the Japanese announced a pol-

Table 1.3. Sectoral Distribution of OECF Loans to Foreign Governments (Commitment Basis), cont.

Mining and Manufacturing	Social Services	Financial Intermediary Loans	Commodity Loans	Other	Total
109.3	96.3	133.8	287.7	54.4	1,091.7
10.0	8.8	12.3	26.4	5.0	100.0
31.6	93.2	70.8	226.2	13.4	846.0
3.7	11.0	8.4	26.7	1.6	100.0
865.9	535.9	276.3	1,688.1	150.6	8,676.0
10.0	6.2	3.2	19.5	1.7	100.0

icy to begin untying their assistance. By 1990, according to Japan's own official statistics, Japanese assistance was 84.5 percent general untied and 15.5 percent LDC untied. No portion of assistance, according to these statistics was completely tied to procurement from Japan (see table 1.4). In addition, according to OECD data, the Japanese aid program is currently one of the most untied of any industrialized country.[17]

Despite these official statistics, many experts in the aid field still conclude that the aid program is a mask for the penetration of Japanese commercial interests into the developing countries; that while officially Japanese aid projects are untied, informal mechanisms still guarantee that Japanese enterprises will win a large slice of the pie. The Japanese respond with statistics showing that the procurement of contracts by Japanese industries has declined significantly in the last decade, from 67 percent in 1986 to 27 percent in 1990.

Moreover, according to the Government of Japan (GOJ), at the request level the tying status is evolving. In 1988,

Figure 1.3. Sectoral Distribution of Japanese Loans to Foreign Governments 1966–1989

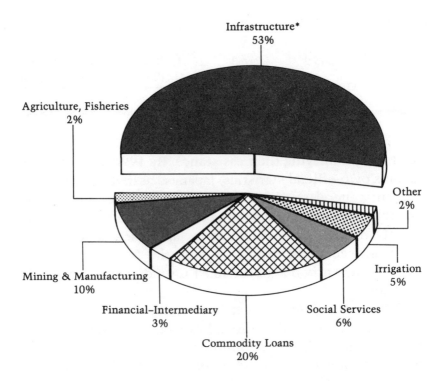

Infrastructure includes Telecommunications, Transportation, Energy
Source: OECF *Annual Report*, 1990

Table 1.4. Procurement Conditions of Japanese Loans to Foreign Governments (Commitments) (%)

Year	Tied	General Untied	LDC Untied	Total
1988	1.0	74.4	24.6	100.0
1989	0.0	85.6	14.4	100.0
1990	0.0	84.5	15.5	100.0

Source: The Overseas Economic Cooperation Fund, July 29, 1991.

the Government of Japan announced to the DAC (Development Assistance Committee) that it would gradually untie the engineering services component of the feasibility studies. According to JICA, these studies are now "generally" LDC untied (specific percentages are not available) and except in rather high per capita income countries such as Korea, Malaysia, Brazil, Thailand, and the Philippines, consultancies are usually LDC untied.

Finally, to counter criticisms that this phase leads to a tied package, the government has recently indicated that up to 50 percent of the consulting contract can be paid as service fees for consultants from other than eligible source countries.[18]

SECTORAL ORIENTATION

The sectoral concentration on assistance for infrastructure or capital projects is also seen as a means for Japanese industry to establish a toehold in the developing countries. The assumption is that this type of assistance, which requires large-scale imports of capital goods, is much easier to "tie" (formally or informally) than, for example, projects focused on basic needs or rural devel-

opment. Infrastructure provides the basis for private investment. Also, if the Japanese aid program is still de facto tied,
this is a primary means for the Japanese to establish and
control markets in the developing countries that are the
recipients of its aid. In addition, infrastructure assistance is
in highly competitive sectors.

While other OECD donors also give assistance for infrastructure, the Japanese are the largest providers of such aid.
In 1989, 43 percent of Japan's assistance was for capital
projects and was primarily in loans rather than grants. This
may be creating additional debt problems in some LDCs
and making sustainable development even more difficult.
For example, in Indonesia, 60 percent of the yen loan assistance goes for debt servicing to Japan.[19] Critics argue that
more assistance should be in the form of grants for basic
needs. Finally, capital projects can have significant impacts
on the environment—a topic that is discussed in chapter
4.

The purpose of this study is to determine who is control-
ling the implementation phase. In the case of Japanese
ODA, this means determining not the agency which is
officially in charge of overseeing specific projects (OECF or
JICA—see chapter 2), but the actual companies who won
contracts—both for loans and for grants. This study origi-
nally began with an attempt to do case studies of the American firms which, according to Japanese data, won Japanese
contracts between 1986 and 1990.

The results on untying and the identification of all such
foreign firms can begin to tell us something about the goals
and motivations of the Japanese aid program. The results
of this search are presented in chapter 3, which concludes
that there are very few cases of non-Japanese companies
winning yen loan financed aid contracts.

The argument presented here suggests that there is a real
disjunction between policy-making and implementation,

particularly for concessional loans. Despite the *official* statistics on untying, the data presented in chapter 3 indicate that the process has not opened up for non-Japanese firms. In fact, it is very clear from an analysis presented in chapter 3 that there is little correspondence between the official statistics on untying and the data provided by this author on foreign procurement. The loan component of Japanese ODA, while officially untied, is at the level of procurement de facto tied. However, contrary to expectation, Japan's Non-Project Grant aid program in Africa appears to be untied and is an unusual example of a foreign assistance program.

The results of this study support the arguments of Orr and Rix that no single motive dominates the Japanese foreign assistance program, and that the objectives as reflected at the policy and implementation level are inconsistent.

On the basis of this analysis, it appears that Japanese motivations at the level of implementation are mixed: in areas where Japan's political, security, and economic interests are paramount, specifically in Asia, a tight control and direction of aid projects is evident. In Africa, where Japan has few strategic interests, the aid program appears to be based more on a desire for international prestige and burden sharing. Japanese assistance appears to be based on two strikingly different policy pillars: a mercantilist strategy to develop markets and a reflection of Japan's desire for international acceptance and prestige.

It is much more difficult to assess effect. As many foreign aid scholars have discovered, evaluating the impact of an aid program is quite murky. It is impossible to develop a singular causal connection between aid and development and the benefit of aid to the donor. Nevertheless, the evidence presented in chapter 4 complements the findings on untying. There is a very close connection between aid and trade at least in the Asian countries that receive the bulk of Japanese assistance. A model that relates aid and trade in infrastructure shows that there is a strong positive relationship between (lagged) aid in infrastructure and infrastructure-based exports from Japan. Aid in infrastructure is helping to finance exports from Japan in infrastructure. The impact of tied assistance (at least for the loan portion of Japan's ODA) on the recipients is difficult to disentangle. There is some evidence to show that this type of assistance —focused on infrastructure—is leading to serious environmental problems in many of the recipient countries. This information is presented in chapter 4.

Japanese industries play perhaps the dominant role in the implementation of Japanese aid policy, at least in Asia. This means that from the developing countries' perspective, the model of development underlying Japanese aid is very different, for example, from the U.S. aid program. It is based, like any donor's aid program, primarily on Japan's culture, experience, and history of economic development, and on a vision of its national interest.

If there is any philosophy underlying Japan's aid program, it is to be found in the notions of self-help and a partnership between the public and private sectors. Economic development in Japan's eyes requires discipline— hence Japan's emphasis on loans that require fiscal discipline—rather than grants. Economic development requires at its initial stage the building of infrastructure that is the foundation for private sector growth. From this follows Japan's emphasis on assistance for capital projects (for infrastructure) rather than on human capital development, such as assistance for basic needs.

Economic development, according to the Japanese, is the result of a tight collaboration between the government and the private sector. This is clearly reflected in Japan's aid program.

The impacts of Japan's tied assistance on Japan and on the recipients are discussed in chapter 4. The implications of these findings for Japan's relationship with the U.S., are analyzed in chapter 5. A summary of the findings and implications is presented in the concluding chapter.

Recipient countries for whom Japan was the Major Donor in 1989

East Asia
1. Brunei
2. China
3. Indonesia
4. Myanmar (Burma)
5. Philippines
6. Singapore
7. Thailand

Southwest Asia
8. Bangladesh
9. Bhutan
10. India
11. Maldives
12. Sri Lanka

Middle East
13. Bahrain
14. Kuwait
15. Saudi Arabia
16. Syria

Africa
17. Ghana
18. Kenya
19. Nigeria
20. Tanzania
21. Zambia

Latin America
22. Brazil
23. Paraguay

Oceania
24. Kiribati
25. Solomon Islands
26. Western Samoa

2

The Structure
and
Implementation
of Japanese
Bilateral
Assistance

BACKGROUND

In the 1960s, Japan was a debtor country and foreign assistance played a major role in its economic development. In 1990, when Japan repaid its last loan from the World Bank (the money had been used to build infrastructure), it had become the world's largest donor of official development assistance (ODA) and the world's largest creditor nation.

ODA has two major components: bilateral and multilateral assistance. Multilateral assistance, which involves contributions to multilateral institutions such as the World Bank and the Asian Development Bank, amounted to $2.186 billion in 1989, or 24.3 percent of total ODA (see table 2.1). Japan has increased such aid dramatically in the last de-

Table 2.1. Japanese Official Development Assistance (ODA) 1989 (Net disbursements, $ millions)

Official Development Assistance	8,965
1. Bilateral Assistance	**6,779**
Grants	3,037
Grant Assistance	1,556
Technical Assistance	1,481
Loans	3,741
2. Multilateral Assistance	**2,186**

Source: Ministry of Foreign Affairs, *Japan's ODA, 1990 Annual Report*, p. 48

cade, becoming one of the largest donors of multilateral assistance.

While Japan's contribution to the multilateral agencies is important and commendable, the focus of this author's research is on bilateral assistance, primarily the loan component of official development assistance, which makes up the bulk of Japan's assistance. For example, $6.779 billion of the $8.965 billion total in 1989, or 75.6 percent of total ODA, was bilateral. It consisted of both loans and grants—loans constituted 55.1 percent of bilateral assistance and 41.7 percent of total ODA. The grant portion of ODA consisted of both grants—44.8 percent of bilateral and 33.8 percent of total ODA—and technical assistance. Technical assistance includes providing experts to LDCs through Japan's Overseas Cooperation Volunteers for training, equipment, and assistance in the preparation of what are called development or feasibility studies.

While Japan was the biggest volume donor in 1989, its aid program received criticism on a number of counts: as a percent of GNP, Japan's program ranks only twelfth among the DAC countries (see table 2.2).

Furthermore, in sharp contrast to other DAC donors, Japanese assistance is denominated primarily in loans rather than grants. In 1989, 55.1 percent of Japan's bilateral assistance was in the form of loans and only 44.8 percent was in grants. When the yen is appreciating, yen-denominated loans are more difficult for the developing country recipients to repay, which leads critics to charge such loans are inappropriate for many recipient countries. Japan's loan fund, implemented through OECF, is extremely large. In 1991, for example, OECF financed a little over $5 billion in loans—making it the third largest development fund in the world, after the World Bank and U.S. A.I.D. The Japanese loan program matches the resources of the Asian Development Bank (ADB), the Inter-American Development Bank (IADB), and the African Development Bank combined. The "hardness" of Japanese bilateral assistance is further indicated in 1988 and 1989 by the fact that Japan ranked last among all DAC countries in what is called the grant element of ODA.

It is important to distinguish between grant aid and the grant element of aid. Grant aid is ODA that does not have to be repaid while the grant element is a function of loans. The latter is a measure of the interest rate, repayment period, and grace period of the loans. There are two reasons for Japan's last-place rank grant element: the small (relative to other DAC countries) portion of aid from grants, and the harder terms of Japanese ODA loans (see table 2.3).

Japan has also been criticized for its regional focus. For security and political reasons, the bulk of Japan's foreign assistance has traditionally gone to the South East Asian countries. This orientation, (reflected in Japan's traditional 70–10–10–10 concentration of 70 percent for Asia, 10 percent for the Middle East, Africa, and Latin America) was modified somewhat in the late 1980s. Both Africa's and

Table 2.2. ODA as a Percent of GNP for DAC Countries, 1989

Country	($ Mil) Amount	Rank	Percent of GNP
Norway	919	1	1.02
Denmark	1,003	2	1.00
Sweden	1,809	3	0.98
Netherlands	2,094	4	0.94
France *	7,467	5	0.78
Finland	705	6	0.63
Belgium	716	7	0.47
Canada	2,302	8	0.44
West Germany	4,953	9	0.41
Italy	3,325	10	0.39
Australia	1,017	11	0.37
Japan	8,958	12	0.32
United Kingdom	2,588	13	0.31
Switzerland	559	14	0.30
Austria	282	15	0.23
New Zealand	87	16	0.22
Ireland	49	17	0.17
United States	7,664	18	0.15

* Includes overseas territories and prefectures
Source: Organization for Economic Cooperation and Development, *Development Cooperation*, 1990.

Table 2.3. ODA Grant Element 1987/88

Country	Rank	Percent
Australia	1	100.0
New Zealand	1	100.0
Ireland	1	100.0
Sweden	1	100.0
Switzerland	5	99.9
Canada	6	99.6
Norway	6	99.6
Denmark	8	99.5
U.K.	9	99.0
Finland	10	97.7
U.S.A.	11	96.9
Netherlands	12	94.1
Belgium	13	94.0*
Italy	14	92.0
France	15	89.3*
West Germany	16	86.1
Austria	17	76.2*
Japan	18	75.4*

* 1987 data
Source: Ministry of Foreign Affairs, *Japan's Official Development Assistance*, 1990, p. 9

Latin America's share of ODA increased during that time. While Africa received just under 10 percent of Japanese ODA in 1987, it increased to 15.3 percent in 1989. Similarly, Latin America's share increased from 6.2 percent in 1988 to 8.3 percent in 1989, a 41 percent increase. These

31

Table 2.4. Japan's Bilateral ODA by Region, 1985–89
(in millions of US dollars; net disbursements)

Year	Total	Asia	Middle East	Africa
1985	$2,577	$1,732	$201	$252
	(100%)	(67.8%)	(7.9%)	(9.9%)
1986	$3,846	$2,494	$340	$418
	(100%)	(64.8%)	(8.8%)	(10.9%)
1987	$5,248	$3,416	$526	$516
	(100%)	(65.1%)	(10.0%)	(9.8%)
1988	$6,422	$4,034	$583	$884
	(100%)	(62.1%)	(9.1%)	(13.8%)
1989	$6,779	$4,240	$368	$1,040
	(100%)	(62.5%)	(5.4%)	(15.3%)

Source: Ministry of Foreign Affairs, *Japan's ODA*, 1990.

increases were offset by a decline in ODA to the Middle East, from 9.1 percent in 1988 to 5.4 percent in 1989 (see table 2.4 and figure 2.1)

The major recipients of Japanese assistance are still Asian countries, however. In 1989, 62.5 percent of Japanese bilateral economic assistance went to that continent, and seven of the top ten recipients of ODA came from Asia (see table 2.5). Moreover, in late 1991, close to a billion dollars in OECF-financed loans to China for infrastructure assistance will tilt the program once again toward the Asian recipients.[1]

Of course the most significant criticism of Japan's aid program has been the assertion of its apparent link to trade and investment. While official statistics indicate that the trade/aid link has developed a crack, if not a break, a perception continues to exist that the aid program is used to

Table 2.4. Japan's Bilateral ODA by Region, 1985–89
(in millions of US dollars; net disbursements), cont.

Latin America	Europe	Oceania	Unallocated
$225	$1	$24	$122
(8.8%)	(0.9%)	(0.9%)	(4.8%)
$317	$2	$55	$221
(8.2%)	(0.1%)	(1.4%)	(5.7%)
$418	$2	$68	$302
(8.0%)	(0.0%)	(1.3%)	(5.8%)
$399	$4	$93	$425
(6.2%)	(0.1%)	(1.4%)	(6.6%)
$563	$11	$98	$458
(8.3%)	(0.2%)	(1.4%)	(6.8%)

advance commercial interests. Why the discrepancy in perception? The reason for such discordancy may well lie in the distinction between policy-formation and project implementation.

Most definitive studies of Japanese aid have looked at *policy-making*. They have concluded that a coherent lack of intent in Japanese foreign aid policy undermines the possibility for a strong aid motive. For example, the complex process of Japanese decision making precludes consistent objectives.[2] Unlike most donor's programs, there is no guiding legislation. Neither is there an accepted nor articulated philosophy underlying Japan's foreign assistance. The lack of an aid philosophy is the outcome of fragmentation at the policy-making level as aid policy is divided among four major bureaucratic actors, all with competing interests. It would be very difficult, then, to define and develop, amidst competing bureaucratic objectives, an overarching, consistent policy that promoted commercial interests.

Figure 2.1. Japan's Bilateral ODA by Region, 1989
U.S. $ Millions

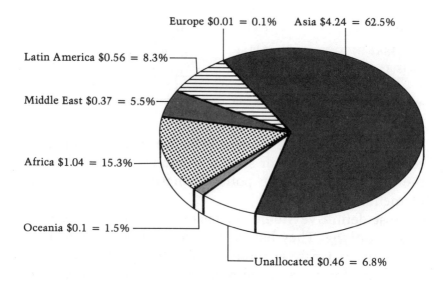

Europe $0.01 = 0.1%   Asia $4.24 = 62.5%

Latin America $0.56 = 8.3%

Middle East $0.37 = 5.5%

Africa $1.04 = 15.3%

Oceania $0.1 = 1.5%

Unallocated $0.46 = 6.8%

Source: Ministry of Foreign Affairs, *Japan's Official Development Assistance*, 1990 Annual Report

ADMINISTRATIVE STRUCTURE

Indeed, the policy-making and administrative structure supporting Japanese bilateral ODA, compared to other DAC donors, is very cumbersome. Three Ministries and one agency (*Yon Schocho Kyogi Taisei*) all with different goals and agendas, shape policy. The Ministry of Finance (MOF), the Ministry of International Trade and Industry (MITI), the Ministry of Foreign Affairs (MOFA) and the Economic Planning Agency (EPA) all have distinct and competing interests and priorities in the making of aid policy. In addition, fourteen other ministries, such as those of Construction and Transportation, also have input into the development financing process.

There are two implementing agencies involved in Japanese ODA, the Overseas Economic Cooperation Fund (OECF) and the Japanese International Cooperation Agency (JICA). These two agencies, however, have little influence on policy-making, with the exception of some cases in which they have a veto power over specific projects. They are more properly viewed as having oversight responsibilities (see figure 2.2).

The impact of bureaucratic politics on the policy process that flows from this organization is well documented by Orr. He concludes that the structure of policy-making prevents a consensus from developing on aid; and that except for agreement that the amount of aid should be increased, there is no consensus on objectives and intentions. Orr thus concludes that aid policy is reactive and open to influence from external actors, particularly the U.S.: "Foreign aid decision-making is highly complex and involves many conflicting interests. Using foreign aid as a tool of Japan, Inc., implies that there is a chairman of the board and consistent policy goals. This study demonstrates quite the contrary."[3]

Table 2.5. Major Recipients of Japan's ODA, 1985–89
(in millions of dollars; net disbursements)

1985		1986		1987	
Country	Amount	Country	Amount	Country	Amount
China	$388	China	$497	Indonesia	$707
Thailand	264	Philippines	438	China	553
Philippines	240	Thailand	260	Philippines	379
Indonesia	161	Bangladesh	248	Bangladesh	334
Burma	154	Burma	244	India	304
Malaysia	126	India	227	Thailand	302
Bangladesh	121	Indonesia	161	Malaysia	276
Pakistan	93	Pakistan	152	Burma	172
Sri Lanka	84	Sri Lanka	127	Turkey	162
Egypt	73	Egypt	126	Pakistan	127

Source: Ministry of Foreign Affairs, *Japan's ODA*, 1990.

Orr's approach, with its strong focus on policy-making, ignores implementation. Yet the lack of policy centralization would leave the system more open to variations at the delivery end. In fact, the potential for those involved in implementation to shape the aid program makes it a rich source for investigation.

Two phases of implementation can influence the decision-making on the project. One is the initial request stage, when projects are identified, and the second is the procurement stage, when decisions are made regarding procurement for specific projects. It is here where the potential exists for Japanese commercial interests to dominate.

Table 2.5. Major Recipients of Japan's ODA, 1985–89
(in millions of dollars; net disbursements), cont.

1988		1989	
Country	Amount	Country	Amount
Indonesia	$985	Indonesia	$1,145
China	674	China	832
Philippines	535	Thailand	489
Thailand	361	Philippines	404
Bangladesh	342	Bangladesh	371
Pakistan	302	India	257
Burma	260	Sri Lanka	185
Sri Lanka	200	Pakistan	177
India	180	Nigeria	166
Egypt	173	Kenya	148

THE REQUEST BASED SYSTEM

Japan's Ministry of Foreign Affairs requires that a request for aid be formally initiated by the potential recipient: "Aid should be used to support self-help efforts by the developing countries, and for this reason its stance with regard to the selection of bilateral aid projects is that such projects should be implemented on the basis of formal requests to the Japanese government from the governments of the recipient nations."[4]

This requirement distinguishes Japanese aid policy from other DAC members. It is the only country offering aid on a request-only basis where the donor funds many of the feasibility studies which lead to the formal request, although the U.S. Trade and Development Program is mov-

37

Figure 2.6. Japanese Bilateral Official Development
Assistance: Administrative Structure

	Policy Making Ministries	Implementing Agency
Loans	Ministry of Finance (MOF) Ministry of Foreign Affairs (MOFA) Ministry of International Trade and Industry (MITI) Economic Planning Agency* (EPA)	Overseas Economic Cooperation Fund (OECF)
Grants	Ministry of Finance (MOF) Ministry of Foreign Affairs (MOFA)	Japanese International Cooperation Agency (JICA)

* Supervises OECF activities

ing in this direction. The development of a request neces-
sitates considerable Japanese involvement, posing the
question of the potential for commercial interests to influence the terms of the request.

The request stage involves eight steps from identification of the project through actual selection. First a project
is "identified" by the recipient country (see figure 2.3).
This is often accomplished with assistance from the Japanese International Cooperation Agency (JICA).

JICA assists in the preparation of many developmental
or feasibility studies, phases two through four. Next consultants are chosen (phase five). The prime consultant or
contractor must be Japanese. Up to one-half of the subcontractors can be foreign. A field survey is then completed by
the consultants (phase six). The results of the survey are

studied in Japan (phase seven) and finally the feasibility study is presented to the appropriate ministries.

It is the request-based nature of the aid program that leads critics to make the case for the influence of Japanese business interests. They point to the Japanese consultants usually used to conduct the feasibility studies to argue that requests are often based more on the needs of Japanese industry than the developing country. Indeed, Japanese consulting companies have strong ties and networks in the developing countries and are often dependent on ODA-related projects for much of their business. Nippon Koei, Japan's largest consulting company depends on ODA for 30 percent of its business.[5] These consultants also know what types of projects will be acceptable to the aid bureaucracy in Japan thus further influencing what type of "request" will be put forth.

The Government of Japan and JICA have countered that this stage of the project cycle is opening up, that foreign consultants are increasingly allowed to be part of the team that prepares this initial request study. An official JICA document describes phases five and six this way:

> In implementing the development study, JICA coordinates the negotiations and confirmation of the Scope of Work (S/W) with the government of the developing country. However, the field survey and analysis study in Japan for the report making are actually conducted by a consultant (company or organization) with abundant experience and specialized expertise. Some 500 consultants are registered with JICA and the most appropriate consultant for the study is selected on the basis of bidding with proposal method.
>
> Although the consultants subject to selection in view of conducting a development study should, in principle, be Japanese nationals, it is permissible to include

Figure 2.3. The Development Study. *The Request Process*

I	**Phase One** **Project Identification**	The host country works with JICA in identifying an appropriate project
II	**Phase Two** **Request**	The recipient country formally requests assistance for the specific project identified in phase one from the Government of Japan. (GOJ)
III	**Phase Three** **Decision on Study Implementation**	Upon receipt of the request, the GOJ instructs JICA to proceed with a study if the project is deemed appropriate.
IV	**Phase Four** **Implementation of Preliminary Study**	JICA dispatches a preliminary study team to the LDC. This team collects basic data and works with the responsible LDC agencies to develop the Scope Of Work (S/W). The S/W is signed during this phase by host country and Japan.
V	**Phase Five** **Selection of Consultant**	JICA selects a consultant from among its registered consultants and a study team is dispatched to the field.

VI	**Phase Six** **Implementation of Field Study**	Based on the S/W, the consultant prepares the inception report, (IC/R). The IC/R describes the methodology for the field survey. The survey is then conducted in the recipient country.
VII	**Phase Seven** **Analysis and Study in Japan**	After the field survey is completed, the consultant presents preliminary results to the GOJ and begins the Draft Final Report (D/FR).
VII	**Phase Eight** **Presentation of Final Report**	Another consultation mission is sent by JICA. Often a seminar in host country is held to share the study results. The LDC has a month after the consultation to comment on the D/FR. When the final report has been agreed upon, the development study is complete.

Source: *Development Study*, JICA (Undated)

foreign nationals in the study team (one quarter of the total number of study team members). In the case of the field survey, domestic consultants with a qualified experience may also be used.[6]

According to JICA then, the prime consultants must be Japanese and registered with JICA. The prime contractor can subcontract up to one-half of the project to a non-Japanese company, which also must be registered with JICA.

The author can only concur that the potential for commercial influence on the direction of a project—in terms of both the type of project and its specifications—is great at this stage. Information that would support or refute this conjecture is almost impossible to obtain. After repeated requests to JICA, this organization released the name of one non-Japanese (American) company which was used in this phase of the project selection. An additional American company was located by the author. These examples are discussed in the next chapter.

FORMAL REQUEST

Next, the project cycle enters the stage of the formal request (see figure 2.4). The developing country submits a formal request for either a loan or a grant, usually to the Japanese embassy in that country. The requests are then examined by the four ministries, with some appraisal being done by one of the two implementing or oversight agencies, OECF and JICA.

Now, OECF and JICA conduct an economic, financial and technical appraisal of the request for the appropriate ministry. It is quite clear that the implementing agencies do not have policy-making powers. It is the four ministries —MOF, MOFA, MITI and EPA—that make the decision on the loans.

BILATERAL LOANS

Once a decision has been made to go ahead with a bilateral loan, a "Prior Notification" is announced. When final agreement is reached on the specifics of the project, that is, the terms and conditions, the two governments sign an Exchange of Notes (E/N). Next, OECF and the recipient country sign a Loan Agreement (L/A), which is the legal document describing in detail "the legal rights and obligations, procurement procedures, disbursement procedures, and the purpose, scope and content of the project."[7]

The next phase of implementation is where decisions are made regarding procurement. Once the Loan Agreement is signed, the recipient country, in principle, makes the procurement decisions. OECF's Annual Report for 1990 describes the process of procurement:

> After the Loan Agreement is signed, the project enters the implementation phase. First, if the loan is to be used for consulting services, the consultants will be selected, using an internationally recognized method, such as the Short List method. Then the materials and equipment needed for the project will be procured, in principle, through international competitive bidding. The announcement of the bidding is made in generally circulated newspapers of the recipient country. Procurement is carried out in line with the OECF's published procurement Guidelines, and the OECF reviews the procurement procedure, documentation, etc.
>
> The Borrower is responsible for the execution of the project or programme, including procurement, However, the OECF monitors implementation of the project, and, where necessary gives advice to the Borrower for smooth implementation of the project or program.

44

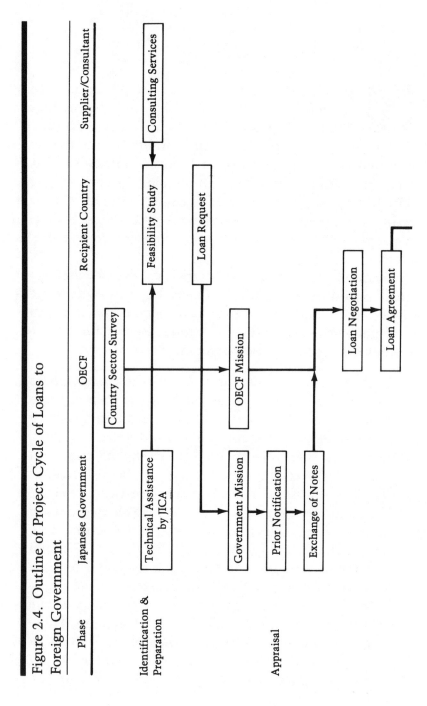

Figure 2.4. Outline of Project Cycle of Loans to Foreign Government

Phase	Japanese Government	OECF	Recipient Country	Supplier/Consultant
Identification & Preparation	Technical Assistance by JICA	Country Sector Survey	Feasibility Study	Consulting Services
			Loan Request	
Appraisal	Government Mission	OECF Mission		
	Prior Notification			
	Exchange of Notes	Loan Negotiation		
		Loan Agreement		

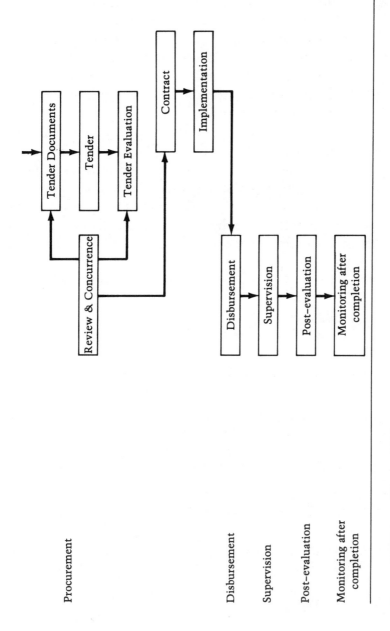

Procurement

- Tender Documents
- Tender
- Tender Evaluation
- Review & Concurrence
- Contract
- Implementation

Disbursement

Supervision

Post-evaluation

Monitoring after completion

Source: OECF *Annual Report*, 1990.

Recently this kind of Monitoring activities has been becoming increasingly important[sic].[8]

Finally, the project cycle moves to evaluation. Usually OECF or JICA conducts the evaluation, although in recent years a few outside experts, including Japanese and non-Japanese scholars and consultants, have been included in this process. The evaluation phase, from the Japanese perspective (and that of other donors) is extremely weak. It will not be treated in this study.

The author chose instead to scrutinize the request level and procurement, through a two year data search, because they are two potential entry points for non-Japanese companies. A survey of successful non-Japanese procurements could illuminate the entire issue of Japan's aid posture and address the question of whether the loop from request through procurement has opened up as much as official statistics would suggest.

3

The
Search for
Non-Japanese
Contractors

BACKGROUND

The Government of Japan's (GOJ) official statistics released in 1991 indicate more than 85 percent of ODA loans are now provided on a general untied basis. In 1989, according to the Ministry of Foreign Affairs, "Japanese companies won contracts for 38 percent of all ODA loans and won only 25 percent of the contracts for general untied ODA loans."[1]

According to the GOJ statistics, the U.S. share of procurement has increased from 2 percent in 1986 to 5 percent in 1989. All other OECD countries have increased their share from 7 percent in 1986 to 16 percent in 1989 (see table 3.1).

Until recently, the GOJ has been unwilling to release the names of companies that won procurement contracts un-

Table 3.1. Actual Procurement by Nationalities of Contractors (Percent)

| | *Nationalities of Contractors* | | | | |
Year	Japan	LDC	OECD*	US	Total
1986	67	24	7	2	100
1987	55	35	7	3	100
1988	43	41	12	4	100
1989	38	41	16	5	100
1990	27	52	16	5	100

* The OECD statistics do not include the figures for the United States.
Source: Ministry of Foreign Affairs, *Japan's ODA, 1990 Annual Report*, p. 21, and OECF (Facsimile, 7/24/91).

der the loan component of Japan's aid program or who had participated in feasibility studies.

In response to repeated requests from the author throughout the spring and summer of 1991, OECF released the names of fourteen non-Japanese companies and one Japanese joint venture that had won procurement contracts over the period 1986–90. During the same period, JICA released the name of one foreign consulting company involved as a subcontractor at the request stage.

Numerous efforts were made to assure the accuracy and completeness of the data released, but repeated requests for additional names were met with assurances that the lists were complete, except for commodities and small loans.

In an additional effort to find more examples of foreign contracts, the author conducted a survey in the summer and fall of 1991 of more than 150 American companies likely to have bid on OECF or JICA projects. The survey (discussed in more detail later) turned up no new contracts.

The overall findings are reviewed below in the context of the loan cycle.

FINDINGS: REQUEST STAGE

For project requests, the aid cycle is apparently very closed to non-Japanese bidders. According to JICA, itself, only one American company, has, over the period from 1986 through 1991 participated in a JICA-funded study, and that was only recently (1991). The firm was Nathan Associates Inc., a consulting company located in Arlington, Virginia which joined as a subcontractor with Nippon Koei Co., Ltd., a Japanese consulting company, to prepare a feasibility study for an export-processing zone in Esmeraldas, Ecuador. According to informal company estimates, Nathan received approximately 10 percent of the contract (a short summary of this project is presented in appendix 3.1). There was insufficient interest among investors to proceed, although one Nathan Associates executive said JICA has expressed hope that AID will proceed with the project!

One additional American firm, Development Alternatives Inc. (DAI), was identified by the author as having participated in five JICA-funded studies. Like Nathan Associates, DAI joined as a subcontractor with Nippon Koei in undertaking feasibility studies in India and Pakistan. DAI has gone one step further than most American firms and set up a one-person office in Tokyo, close to a $100,000 yearly investment, to tap the Japanese aid market. According to the founder of this firm, American firms who are interested in Japanese aid projects must be willing to make a long-term commitment to understanding the aid process.[2]

Several other American firms were reported to have participated in JICA-funded studies through subcontracting relationships with Japanese firms. No other examples, however, could be confirmed. The survey of American companies indicated that a common perception is that the system is a closed loop; that although the Japanese aid program has become more open on paper, it is closed to non-Japanese companies in practice.

Asked why it appears that foreign companies have made very few inroads into the critical, initial stage when a project is defined, JICA and OECF officials respond that American companies, in particular, have not made the effort to establish themselves with a Japanese consulting firm. Their argument is that the process is open for companies who make the effort. There is probably some truth to this, as reflected in some comments to the effect that the Japanese aid market is "too difficult to crack" and it is "rigged against outsiders." Yet if American firms like DAI do make more of an effort at this initial stage and develop working relationships with their Japanese counterparts, it is still unclear whether this effort would result in payoffs. However, without gaining a toehold at the initial request stage, it is very unlikely that non-Japanese companies will win bids at the procurement stage.

PROCUREMENT PHASE: FINDINGS

The next potential entry point, both for Japanese and non-Japanese businesses to become involved, is the procurement stage. This is the stage, obviously, where the bulk of the aid money is spent, and the point, according to the Government of Japan, where the process has become open to non-Japanese companies. According to table 3.1, the share of non-Japanese contractors winning procurement bids has increased quite dramatically since 1986.

Who are the companies who have won ODA loan contracts? It became clear early on in the research that it was going to be very difficult to find them. Documents recently released by OECF to the author on companies which won procurement contracts after September 1986, listed no American company. One American company, De Leuw, Cather International Ltd. (DCIL), has worked in association with a Thai-based firm, Thai-DCI Co. Ltd. Since this is a significant finding, it is important to quote OECF staff exactly:

> The list of contracts [that I was able to provide you] was drawn from that relatively small portion which currently meets the criteria for publication, i.e., contracts financed by loan agreements (L/As) whose exchange of notes (E/N) was concluded after September 1986. Generally, the time lag between E/N and tender is more than one year. As a result, the portion eligible to be made public is expected to increase substantially in coming years. Information about the remaining contracts is, unfortunately, restricted by Government policy.[3]

The information released by OECF showed fourteen non-Japanese companies and one Swedish-Japanese joint venture company as having won parts of nine OECF-financed projects in the developing countries from 1986 through 1990. The corporations are listed in table 3.2 along with the nationality of each company and the location of the development project. Appendix 3.2 contains a short description of each company. The projects, themselves, are listed by number and are described in table 3.3 below. The recently published 1991 *OECF Annual Report* listed some additional foreign corporations (see Epilogue). The aggregate statistics presented in table 3.5 include these companies' procurement.

It is clear there is little correspondence between the offi-

Table 3.2. Non-Japanese Corporations Involved in OECF Financed ODA Projects

#	Year	Recipient Country	Contractor	Nationality of Contractor
1.	1987	Thailand	Daewoo (1)	Korea
2.	1987	Pakistan	National Engineering Services, Pakistan (2)	Pakistan
3.	1988	Malaysia	MMC Gas SDN, BHD (3) BHD Confab Indust SA (4) Petrobus Comercio Int. SA (5) Sabdna-Hamison, Sdn, Bhd. (6)	Malaysia Brazil/Malaysia
4.	1988	Thailand	Telefonakiebolaket (7) Les Cables de Lyon (8) Kabel B.V. (9)	Sweden/Japan France Netherlands
5.	1988	Thailand	Telefonaktiebolaget LM Ericsson (10) Les Cables de Lyon (8) Association Engineering and Philips Electrical Co. of Thailand (11)	Sweden France Netherlands/Thai
6.	1989	Thailand	Elin Energie-Versorgung Gesellschaft MBH (12)	German
7.	1990	Thailand	Thai DCI Co. (13)	Thai
8.	1990	Sri Lanka	W.S. Atkins Int. (14)	UK
9.	1990	Malaysia	Transmark (15)	UK

Source: OECF, Washington office. Facsimile 7/10/1991.

Table 3.3. Project Descriptions

Project #	Loan Amount ($000)	Loan Amount (¥000s)	Name of Project
1.	29,826	3,937	Passenger Coaches Procurement
2.	115,909	15,300	Bin Qasim Thermal Power Station Expansion
3.	345,537	42,000	Peninsular Gas Utilization (II)
4.	119,985	24,296	Telephone Network Expansion (I-2)
5.	85,734	10,421	Telephone Network Expansion (Local Cable Network)
6.	16,976	2,425	Bhumibol Hydro Power Plant Rehabilitation
7.	94,397	12,517	Road Improvement Program for Three Major Routes
8.	2,255	299	Greater Colombo Drainage System Rehabilitation
9.	146,637	19,444	Malayan Railway Improvement

Source: OECF, Washington office. Facsimile 7/10/1991.

cial GOJ statistics on procurement presented in table 3.1 and the information garnered from OECF and presented in tables 3.2 and 3.3.

According to the statistics presented in table 3.4 and figure 3.1 below, the share of non-Japanese companies winning OECF financed contracts has increased substantially since 1986.

By collapsing the three categories of non-Japanese contractors (LDC, OECD and US) from table 3.1 into one category

Table 3.4. Procurement by Nationalities of Contractors
(Percent)

| Year | Nationalities of Contractors | | Total |
	Japanese	Non-Japanese	
1986	67	33	100
1987	55	45	100
1988	43	57	100
1989	38	62	100
1990	27	73	100

Source: Original data source from: Government of Japan, July 27, 1991 and OECF
(Facsimile, 7/24/91).

—procurement by non-Japanese contractors—we see that procurement by non-Japanese contractors would have had to increase from 33 percent in 1986 to 73 percent in 1990 (see table 3.4 and figure 3.1).

The discrepancy is most apparent when the loan amounts from table 3.1 are converted into percentages and measured against overall loans for those years. Each of the yen amounts from table 3.3 were converted into dollars. These amounts, listed in table 3.5 (and figure 3.2) below, are then converted into percentages based on total loans for that year. The gap between the statistics of table 3.4 and those of table 3.5 is glaring. Instead of a 33 percent procurement rate for non-Japanese companies in 1986, there was no procurement by foreign firms in that year. Similarly, in 1990, $3.9 billion of Japanese aid money was in the form of loans and 6.47% went to foreign contractors. The largest amount of non-Japanese procurement actually occurred in 1988 when 25.4% of all OECF loans, in contrast to the 57% of table 3.4, were won by non-Japanese firms. When all joint ventures are included, the statistics improve somewhat to 9.72% in 1987; 49.3% in 1988, 16.02% in 1989, and 8.36% in 1990.

Figure 3.1. Procurement by Nationalities of Contractors (%)

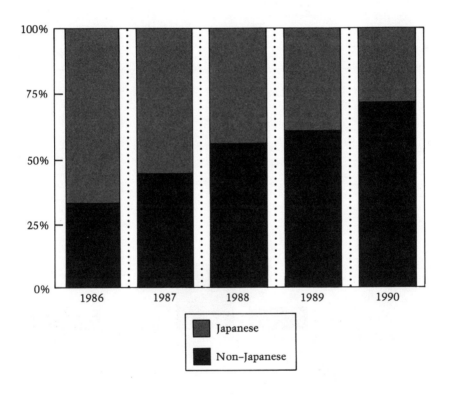

Source: Ministry of Foreign Affairs, *Japan's ODA*, 1990, Annual Report

Figure 3.2. Foreign Procurement (%) As a Proportion of Bilateral Loans

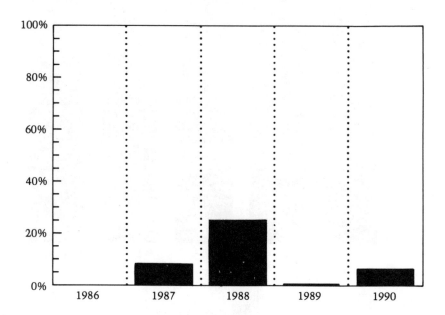

Source: Ministry of Foreign Affairs, *Japan's ODA*, Various Years; OECF, 1991

Table 3.5. Foreign Procurement (Amounts and Percent compared to ODA in loans)

		(US $000)	
Year	Loans (US $)	Foreign Procurement (US $)	% of Foreign Procurement
1986	2,143,000	0	0
1987	3,027,000	254,132	8.39
1988	3,514,000	893,196	25.4
1989	3,741,000	59,706	1.59
1990	3,920,000	253,859	6.47

Sources: Government of Japan, July 27, 1991, OECF (Facsimile, 7/24/91) and Ministry of Foreign Affairs, *Japan's Bilateral ODA*, Various Years; OECF 1991 *Annual Report*.

SURVEY

Surprised by the sparse lists provided by GOJ, the author conducted a survey of more than 150 American firms. These companies had sent representatives to two Agency for International Development (A.I.D.)-sponsored conferences on Japanese foreign assistance and so were likely to have bid on OECF and JICA projects. The survey asked whether the company had ever bid on and/or won an OECF or JICA financed aid project. The results of the survey indicated that few companies had bid and that no firm surveyed had ever won an OECF or JICA-financed contract.

Information released from the Embassy of Japan in Washington D.C. in the summer of 1992 listed three companies, additional to the OECF data, as having successfully bid on OECF financed projects in fiscal 1989. All three were American firms: AT&T International, Robbins and

Myers Inc., and Amico Trading, Inc. This information was either unsupported or contradicted.[4] Finally, several experts reported that a Thai-American joint venture had won an OECF-financed project for part of a new airport terminal in Bangkok. This also proved to be incorrect.[5] According to the *Financial Times* in 1989 the General Electric Company of the United Kingdom won a 37 million pounds order for part of the railway system in Thailand, beating out Mitsui of Japan and an American firm. The 1991 OECF *Annual Report* also lists one additional American firm, Morrison Knudsen Engineers, as having participated in a joint venture with eight partners in a project in Indonesia in 1989. General Electric in Mexico and Malaysia won a total of $50 million in locomotive procurement in 1990 and more recently, in December 1991, the American firm DCIL won. Recently, in December 1991, the American firm DCIL did win part of an OECF-financed project in the Philippines, the South Luzon Expressway Extension Project. Consulting services are being provided by DCIL in association with DCCD Engineering Corporation and Demcor, Inc., both Philippine-based companies. Two Japanese firms, Katahira and Engineers International and Nippon Engineering Consultants Co., Ltd. are also partners in the project. DCIL is considered the leader.

Obviously there is a large discrepancy between table 3.4 and the company specific data presented in tables 3.2 and 3.3 and their corresponding aggregate statistics presented in table 3.5. What is to account for it? The official explanation is that all data on foreign procurement have not been released. Specifically foreign contractors for small projects, defined as less than 100 million yen, and commodity loans are not included in the released names. A chart drawn by an OECF representative is presented in figure 3.3.

This chart purports to explain the gap between the aggregate data in tables 3.1 and 3.4 and the company specific data presented in tables 3.2 and 3.3. According to this very rough diagram, small contracts and commodity loans make up the difference between the two sets of statistics—a gap that merely indicates more data on foreign procurement will be released in the near future. Beginning in 1991 the OECF annual report lists the names of foreign contractors.

It is unlikely that the remaining percentages could be made up by either of these two categories. During the period from 1966 through 1989, commodity loans averaged 19.5 percent per year. While this category has been increasing in recent years, reaching a high of 26.7 percent in 1989, even if all commodity loans had been won by foreign contractors, the statistics from tables 3.4 and 3.5 would still not match. While information on small contracts and commodity loans could fill out the picture, the data released and uncovered by this study show that for the years 1986–90, the share of non-Japanese corportions does not match the data in table 3.4.

It is therefore clear that in the overall aid cycle the loop from feasibility study to procurement is still inaccessible to non-Japanese companies and that despite aggregate statistics on untying, foreign companies are making very few inroads into the Japanese-financed loan component of the aid program.

It appears then that Japanese aid, at least that financed through concessional loans, is *effectively* tied to purchases in Japan. That is to say, informal, rather than formal restrictions apparently exist between the donor and recipient countries receiving the aid. Bhagwati has termed this informal or indirect tying:

> There is little doubt that informal tying operates with efficiency in many cases. This can take the form of impressing on the recipient country that any departures from *de facto* tying in purchases would be short-

Figure 3.3. Proportion of Total Contracts Agreed to by OECF

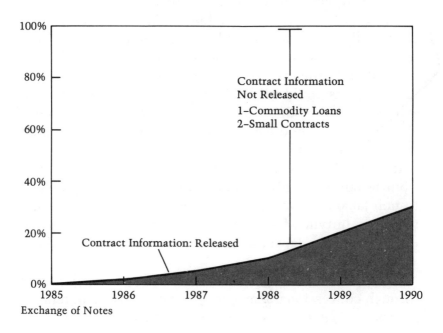

Contract Information
Not Released
1–Commodity Loans
2–Small Contracts

Contract Information: Released

Exchange of Notes

Source: OECF, 1991.

sighted and would cause difficulties in continuing or even granting aid. . . . Another method, which seems to have gained ground whenever formal and informal restrictions have been considered undiplomatic, is to finance only those commodities and/or projects where the donor country is considered to have a decided advantage in tendering or supplying the specified items."

This policy can be implemented by letting it be known generally and informally that the chance of securing aid would improve if the project or commodities required were "suitably chosen" so as to result in directly identifiable imports from the donor despite competitive tendering.[6]

Anecdotal information supports this description of the aid process. As one American executive interviewed for this study recounts: "The host country respects the wishes of OECF whether explicit or implicit. Implicit in OECF projects is the notion that Japanese firms should be involved, at least in some small way, even though the project is so called general untied. The host countries in some cases insist on this even though OECF regulations do not require it."[7]

These findings show that the loan component of Japanese aid is effectively tied to purchases from Japan. The hypothesis that aid and trade are linked, specifically that aid is used to develop markets for future trade, is explored in the next chapter.

First, however, it is important to briefly take up Japan's grant aid program in Africa, where the picture here is somewhat different. Surprisingly, part of Japan's grant aid program in Africa has been turned over to two non-Japanese agents for implementation.

NON-PROJECT GRANT AID
IN AFRICA

In 1987, Japan began a program in Sub-Saharan Africa, unique among the DAC countries, which they called the Japanese Non-Project Grant Aid program. An unusual program, it is untied and is implemented by two non-Japanese organizations: British Crown Agents and the United Nations Development Program (UNDP).

Funding for this program comes directly from the Grant Aid Division of the Economic Cooperation Bureau in the Ministry of Foreign Affairs. There is no involvement of either OECF or JICA. Unlike the bulk of the assistance financed by OECF, this program is not for infrastructure-type project assistance but primarily for commodity assistance such as spare parts and vehicles.

Crown Agents, the world's largest public-sector procurement agency, is in charge of one-half of the project, UNDP, the other half. For Africa, the program is a large one in volume. During the first three-year phase (1988–91), $500 million was disbursed in 26 countries in Sub-Saharan Africa. The second three-year phase (1991–1994) involves $600 million in disbursements and the regional focus has been broadened to include countries in South America and Asia. (Appendix 3.3 lists the countries of origin for goods procured through Crown Agents. Appendices four and five contain a list of the recipient countries and six breaks out the categories of goods procured under this program.)

This program, like OECF-financed loans, is "request based." Procurement decisions are made by the recipient countries in conjunction with the Government of Japan: "The actual decision on the requirements to be financed from the Grants is made by the Recipient Governments according to their needs and advised to the Government of

Table 3.6. Procurement Share by Nationality Crown Agents
Share (Approximately ½) 1988–1991

Japan	UK	Germany	U.S.	Italy
33.7	16.5	7.95	6.6	2.24

Source: Crown Agents, Facsimile, 7/19/1991.

Japan. From Crown Agents point of view, and I am sure that this is equally so for the UNDP, each case is evaluated individually from the point of view of optimizing the benefit to the recipient by achieving the best value for money between competing products."[8]

According to Crown Agents, 6,500 tenders for products have been issued to more than 45 countries since 1988. Crown Agents' statistics also indicate, however, that the bulk of the procurement materials have come, so far, from Japan. The high Japanese procurement rate according to Crown Agents reflects the "high proportion of competitively produced vehicles"[9] manufactured in Japan.

Crown Agents ameliorate that picture of the Japanese share, however, by raising an interesting point about the U.S. share. They estimate it is considerably understated because overseas production by subsidiaries is usually tabulated (if at all) in host country statistics:[10] "There is a significant element of disguise in the US share, insofar as American companies are heavily into overseas production by subsidiaries or licensees. For instance, one of Crown Agents' largest individual orders in the programme was for five American locomotives: But they were actually manufactured by the US company's plant in Brazil and are thus not included in the above 6.6 percent."[11]

UNDP's portion of this grant program began in 1988 with one country and an $11.7 million grant and grew to include 18 countries totaling $273.8 million in grant assis-

Table 3.7. Procurement Share by Nationality UNDP Share
(½) 1988–1991

Japan	France	UK	Germany	Italy
19.4	19.8	13.6	6.3	5.8

Source: Crown Agents, Facsimile, 7/19/1991.

tance by 1991. In 1989 a special unit within the United Nations Development Programme, The Japanese Procurement Programme, was established to implement this program. Like Crown Agents procurement, goods procured under UNDP's programme include commodities as diverse as buses, fishing nets, tents, hand tools, and vaccines.[12]

The UNDP figures are interesting from a number of angles. The French share is the largest. This is due in great part to the fact that UNDP's portion of the grant covers mostly Francophone countries in Africa. Also, according to Crown Agents, "these figures fluctuate and can be affected significantly by a few large orders."[13]

CONCLUSION

The contrast between OECF-financed projects and the grant aid program in Africa is worth noting. The former is effectively tied and the latter appears to be untied and administered by nongovernmental organizations. One conclusion that can be drawn from these findings is that in countries where Japanese economic interests are paramount, particularly in Asia, Japanese aid is effectively tied. Contrariwise, in regions where Japan's interests are not well developed, such as in Africa, aid appears to be unrelated to commercial interests.

The impacts of these findings—particularly those related to OECF loan projects on the donor and recipient countries—are addressed in chapter 4.

APPENDIX 3.1

Company Specific Information: Feasibility study

The feasibility study described in this chapter involved a market survey of potential investors for an export processing zone in Esmeraldas, Ecuador. The survey of potential investors in North America and Mexico was conducted by Nathan Associates. Nippon Koei conducted market surveys in Japan and Ecuador. According to executives at Nathan Associates, the working relationship with Nippon Koei was a very good one. These same executives were surprised that Nippon Koei had chosen them. They had never done business with Nippon Koei before, but had, several years beforehand, introduced themselves to Nippon Koei officials in Tokyo.

Company Descriptions: Procurement Phase

1. **Daewoo** is a major South Korean Corporation that manufactures industrial and construction equipment, electronics, passenger cars, and commercial vehicles.
2. **National Engineering Services, Pakistan,** is a large state-owned (Pakistani) corporation.
3. **MMC Gas SDN:** MMC is the Malaysia Mining Corporation Berhad. Incorporated in Malaysia, this corporation is involved in all phases of mining operations: engineering, exploration, management, and marketing.
4. **BHD Confab Industries,** the company listed as having won a bid in Malaysia in 1988, could not be located in any standard reference materials.

5. **Petrobus Comercio:** Petroleo Brasileiro S.A. Petrobus is a Brazilian based company involved with oil exploration and production.

6. **Sabdna-Hamison Sdn. Bhd,** the company listed as having won a bid in Malaysia in 1988, could not be located in any standard reference materials.

7. **Telefonakiebolaket,** the Swedish/Japanese company listed as winning a bid in Thailand in 1988, could not be located.

8. **Les Cables de Leon** is a subsidiary of a French-owned company, Alcatel N.V. Alcatel is engaged in public communications systems including digital switching systems, cable and fiber optic transmission networks, and radio and satellite transmission systems. Les Cables de Leon, headquartered in Clichy, France, manufactures power and communications cables.

9. **Kabel B.V.,** the company from the Netherlands listed as winning a bid in Thailand in 1988, could not be located.

10. **Telefonaktiebolaget, LM Ericsson** is a major Swedish company involved with advanced telecommunications and electronic defense systems.

11. **Association Engineering and Phillips Electrical Company of Thailand,** could not be found in any standard reference text.

12. **Elin Energie Versorgung Gesellschaft MBH,** the German company listed as winning a bid in Thailand, in 1989, could not be located.

13. **Thai-DCI Co., Ltd.** is a Thai-based engineering consulting firm. Parsons Polytech of Japan and De Leuw, Cather International, Ltd. (DCIL) worked in association with Thai-DCI on the road improvement project and another highway related project. DCIL is actually a subsidiary of a large American engineering and construction management company based in Pasadena, California, The Parson Corporation. Par-

sons also owns 49 percent of Parsons Polytech of Japan; Shimizu, a large Japanese construction contractor, owns the other 51 percent. (The Parsons Corporation purchased Parsons Polytech in order to give Parsons entry into the Japanese market.) These OECF-financed projects in Thailand involve construction supervision services and assistance to the Department of Highways. Parsons Polytech provided the project manager for the two contracts. One of the reasons cited for DCIL's success in winning these contracts is that they became involved in the projects at a very early stage and actually formed the LDC/U.S./Japanese team to bid on the project.

14. **W.S. Atkins Ltd.** is a British consulting company involved in the areas of engineering, architecture, planning and management.
15. **Transmark** is a British corporation involved in engineering and construction projects.

    Additional companies were listed in the 1991 *OECF Annual Report.* That list appears in the Epilogue.

Reference books examined were:

- Moody's International, 1990 Vols. 1–2;
- International Directory of Corporate Affiliations, 1990;
- *Europe's 15,000 Largest Companies* (Duns Marketing Service), 1989;
- *Principal International Business,* 1989 Dun and Bradstreet; and
- the U.S. Department of Commerce, CD-Rom, World Scope.

Origin of Goods,
by Crown Agents

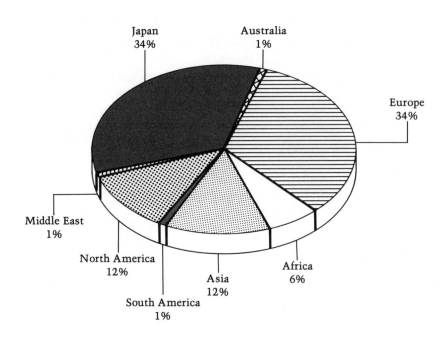

Source: Crown Agents, 1991

Japanese Grant Aid in Africa: Japanese Procurement Programme

Countries and Amounts Procured by the United Nations
Development Programme

Country	Yen Grant Amount	U.S. Dollar Total Including Interest
FY 1987/88		
Cote d'Ivoire 1	2.0 billion	13.8 million
Niger	1.5 billion	12.6 million
Somalia	.9 billion	6.6 million
FY 1988/89		
Guinea	.5 billion	3.8 million
Madagascar	3.5 billion	26.5 million

Countries and Amounts Procured by the United Nations Development Programme, cont.

Country	Yen Grant Amount	U.S. Dollar Total Including Interest
Mauritania	.5 billion	3.7 million
Senegal [1]	2.5 billion	17.4 million
Togo	.7 billion	5.0 million
Zaire	3.5 billion	26.0 million
FY 1989/90		
Benin	.7 billion	5.2 million
Central African Republic	.3 billion	2.3 million
Cote d'Ivoire- 2nd Grant [1]	1.7 billion	12.9 million
Mali	.5 billion	3.8 million
Niger-2nd Grant	1.5 billion	10.8 million
Togo-2nd Grant	.5 billion	3.9 million
FY 1990/91		
Benin-2nd Grant	.9 billion	6.5 million
Bolivia	.9 billion	6.5 million
Guinea-2nd Grant	.5 billion	3.7 million
Honduras	.5 billion	3.6 million
Madagascar 2nd Grant	3.5 billion	25.4 million
Mauritania 2nd Grant	.5 billion	3.6 million
Nicaragua	.9 billion	6.5 million
Senegal 2nd Grant [1]	2.5 billion	18.8 million

Countries and Amounts Procured by the United Nations Development Programme, cont.

Country	Yen Grant Amount	U.S. Dollar Total Including Interest
FY 1991/92		
Burkina Faso	.3 billion	2.2 million
Cameroon	.9 billion	6.5 million
Central African Republic-2nd Grant	.5 billion	3.6 million
Cote d'Ivoire 3rd Grant	2.5 billion	18.1 million
Mongolia	2.0 billion	14.5 million
Grant Total	37.2 billion	273.8 million

Source: Facsimile: Karen Dreher, United Nations Procurement Programme, Office for Project Services, October 9, 1991.

1. Country for which UNDP is serving only as verification/certification agent.
2. Yen 26 billion not including grants to Cote d'Ivoire and Senegal.
3. $192.8 million not including grants to Cote d'Ivoire and Senegal.

Japanese Grant Aid in Africa: Japanese Procurement Programme

Countries and Amounts Procured by Crown Agents
(Only Years 1990–92)

Country	Yen Grant Amount	U.S. Dollar Total
FY 1990/91		
Burundi	.3 billion	2.26 million
Ghana	1.5 billion	11.28 million
Guinea Bissau	.3 billion	2.26 million
Malawi	.3 billion	2.26 million
Mozambique	1.50 billion	11.28 million
Nigeria	2.50 billion	18.80 million

Countries and Amounts Procured by Crown Agents (Only Years 1990–92), cont.

Rwanda	.5 billion	3.76 million
Tanzania	2.0 billion	15.04 million
Uganda	.5 billion	3.76 million
Zambia	3.5 billion	26.32 million
Zimbabwe	1.5 billion	11.28 million
Subtotal	14.40 billion	108.27 million
FY 1991/92		
Peru	3.5 billion	26.32 million
Philippines	3.5 billion	26.32 million
Zambia	3.5 billion	26.32 million
Gambia	.3 billion	2.26 million
Subtotal	10.8 billion	81.20 million
Grand Total	25.20 billion	189.47 million

Source: Japanese Non-Project Aid. Crown Agents Financial Status Report, May 30, 1991.

Japanese Non Project Grant Aid, 1989 and 1990: Commodities Purchased by Crown Agents

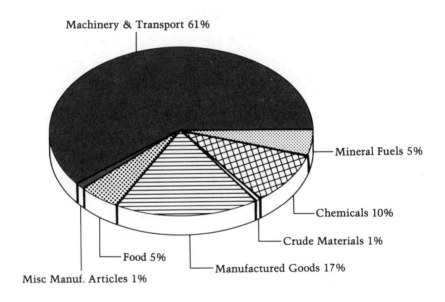

Machinery & Transport 61%

Mineral Fuels 5%

Chemicals 10%

Crude Materials 1%

Manufactured Goods 17%

Food 5%

Misc Manuf. Articles 1%

Source: Crown Agents, 1991

Japanese Non Project Aid, 1988 and 1989 Commodities Through UNDP in Africa

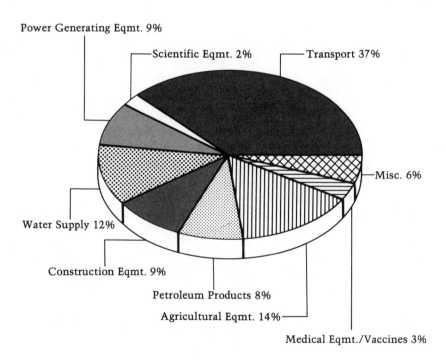

Power Generating Eqmt. 9%

Scientific Eqmt. 2%

Transport 37%

Misc. 6%

Water Supply 12%

Construction Eqmt. 9%

Petroleum Products 8%

Agricultural Eqmt. 14%

Medical Eqmt./Vaccines 3%

Source: UNDP, 1991

4

Tied Aid and Its Outcome for the Donor— and the Recipient

The findings from chapter 3 show that the loan component of Japanese aid is effectively tied to purchases from Japan. What is the impact of this tied aid both on the donor and the recipient countries?

TIED AID: IMPACT ON THE DONOR

There are both economic and political outcomes sought by a donor in tying its assistance. The desired political effect may include promoting and protecting its security concerns as well as its historical and cultural ties. Each donor's aid reflects a different mix of these concerns. In the case of Japan, security concerns are primarily economic in nature. Japan's regional aid bias toward the Asian countries reflects its security goals.

Purely economic motives for tying aid can be to increase exports and to reduce the potentially negative impact of aid on the donor's balance of payments. Aid tied to procurement from the donor reduces such risk.[1] While most empirical studies have concluded that tied aid has an almost negligible impact on a country's balance of payments, these studies have also concluded that tied aid can have a significant impact on the trade balance of specific sectors or firms.[2] Two additional hypotheses have been developed to explain why countries tie aid: (1) to protect weak industries; (2) to promote strong industries. Empirical research in this area, while scanty, has tended to support the second hypothesis, that aid is channeled to sectors where donors have a comparative advantage.[3]

To test the hypothesis that aid is channeled to support and promote strong industries, the author studied statistics for the years 1982–89 in order to compare Japanese ODA for infrastructure with exports from the same period. Six countries—Indonesia, Malaysia, the Philippines, Thailand, China and Korea—all of them major recipients of Japanese ODA were studied The sample size was restricted to these years because of difficulties in locating data for the variables discussed below.

Infrastructure was chosen because most of Japanese loans in general, and specifically to these countries, fall under that category. Moreover, Japanese firms have a comparative advantage in several of the infrastructure-related sectors, including telecommunications.

Data on ODA loans by sector were available from the yearly Japanese statistics on ODA published by the Ministry of Foreign Affairs. Each country is listed in this document along with specific projects and programs funded for that year. Trade data, however, are not available at this level of specificity. The annual White Paper on International Trade published by MITI lists exports by several categories that match the aid data, namely trade in telecommunications and construction for infrastructure-related projects. For each of the six countries, aid-financed projects in any of the trade-related categories were identified and then converted into dollars. For the years 1982 through 1989 data were then compiled for aid and trade in infrastructure in these two categories: telecommunications and construction for infrastructure. A full discussion of the conclusions appears in appendix 4.1. While the data obviously underestimate the total volume of aid and trade in infrastructure, it was necessary to reduce the variables to these categories to achieve comparability.

A regression model was built to test the hypothesis that aid in infrastructure and trade in infrastructure are positively related. It is unlikely that aid in the concurrent year with trade would be positively related.[4] The assumption here is that it takes at least one year for aid procurement decisions to be made and funds disbursed. Therefore, aid in infrastructure would be "lagged" one year.

The results of the regression analysis indicate that aid in infrastructure is a significant predictor of trade in infrastructure, supporting a hypothesis that aid literally lays the infrastructure for trade in subsequent years.

The model is very simple and preliminary. A more comprehensive model would include such variables as real interest rates, inflation rates, a measure of political stability, labor costs and private investment.

The multiple regression model may overestimate the impact of aid in infrastructure on exports. However, a convincing methodology has yet to be developed for factoring out exports financed through aid or exports that would have been purchased anyway, without the assistance.

Even with these limitations, however, these data do indicate that there is a positive relationship between aid, at least in infrastructure, and trade in infrastructure—sectors

where Japan has a comparative advantage. To fully understand the relationship between these variables, a more en-
compassing model would need to be built, and case studies
of individual countries conducted.

TIED AID: IMPACT ON
THE RECIPIENTS

There are a number of potential costs of tied aid—
both direct and indirect—on the recipient countries. The primary effect hypothesized is a higher
commodity price due to monopolistic pricing. According to
Jepma, "theoretically, if the number of potential suppliers
is limited, there is greater probability that the price of the
commodity will be higher due to monopolistic pricing,
than under conditions of perfect competition. It is, therefore generally assumed that tying of aid will raise the price
of the commodities delivered, since in the absence of full
international competition, the supplier will tend to exploit
the situation."[5]

A number of indirect costs have also been identified,
including:

- a preference accorded to projects that require major
  imports in areas of particular export interest to the
  donor;
- a corresponding bias against projects and programmes
  with low import content such as rural development
  projects, and in particular those involving local cost
  financing;
- a privileged place accorded to commercially interesting projects; and
- impaired credibility of donors in the development policy dialogue with recipients.[6]

But these hypotheses, like the impact of tied aid on the donor, have received very little empirical attention. It is extremely difficult to test any of the propositions, particularly those related to increased costs. Empirical data on the price of products financed by ODA is almost nonexistent. According to a recent report in this area, "price information is normally kept confidential by competitors bidding for the same project . . . price data may be difficult to compare as the deliveries are often not homogeneous products . . . bribing may make price competition irrelevant and thus price information obtained of no value."[7]

Bhagwati developed one way of inferring the cost of tied aid. He examined the range of bids for World Bank and International Development Association (IDA) projects for the period 1960–66. He discovered that the potential "excess cost of tying is in the order of 50 percent, if the average excess amount of the 'high bids' over the successful ones is considered an accurate indicator. In addition, more than 60 percent of the value of contracts awarded was characterized by potential excess costs of greater than 30 percent."[8] Another way to assess the costs of tied aid is to compare the price of exports not financed through ODA to ODA-financed commodities. Several studies have found the following:

- A Norwegian study concluded that fertilizer grants provided by a variety of donors were at price levels "10–20 percent above world market prices."[9]
- A study by UNCTAD showed tied aid increased costs of items from 3 to 30 percent.[10]
- In a 1970 study, Bhagwati estimated the average cost of tied aid to be between 20 and 25 percent.[11]
- A 1991 study by Jepma estimated that tied aid may increase the cost to the recipients by 20 to 30 percent.[12]

However, Jepma has indicated that one should be cautious about assuming that tied aid necessarily leads to in-

creased costs. According to Jepma, several factors may reduce the potential for cost-raising.

> In the first place, the supplier of the aid-financed com-
> modity may be the most cost-effective one, charging
> the lowest price of all suppliers, and since empirical
> evidence suggests that countries tend to supply the
> recipients with commodities corresponding to their
> areas of comparative advantage, the probability of fair
> prices increases. In the second place, even if procure-
> ment is restricted to the donor country, this does not
> preclude a certain amount of competition among na-
> tional suppliers, especially if the country is rather large.
> This obviously depends upon procurement proce-
> dures. In the third place, a supplier may consider the
> aid-financed exports as a way of entering the recipi-
> ent's market and thus will offer his products at highly
> competitive prices. Finally, the donor country's gov-
> ernment may be an important customer of the sup-
> plier so that the latter cannot afford to make a
> "bad impression" with respect to the aid-financed
> deliveries.[13]

Some anecdotal data do support the hypothesis that Japanese ODA increases the costs for recipient countries. In
1980, when Japan financed an integrated steel mill project
in one northeast Asian country, materials were "procured
at prices two to five times higher than usual export prices."[14]
In addition, an economics professor at Thamassat University in Thailand has concluded that because of procurement conditions and the appreciation of the yen, "Thailand
ends up being able to use only 25 percent of what it bor-
rows, especially when this country's income is in U.S.
dollars while loans must be repaid in yen."[15] Without very
specific data on both aid projects and exports, it is certainly
impossible to estimate the financial costs of tied aid.

Excessive prices are only one of the potential costs of tied aid. If it reduces the recipient's choice in determining development projects, it lessens the opportunity for projects most advantageous to the recipients. The following are good examples of inappropriate "development" assistance projects. In 1988, Japan's Ministry of Transport announced a plan, the Holiday Village Project, to develop tourist spots for Japanese tourists in Third World countries using both ODA and private funds. While ODA was used only for the feasibility studies, the plan has been severely criticized as a misuse of development funds. Despite such criticisms, the project was launched in May of 1990 and sites are being surveyed in Malaysia, China, Thailand, and Mexico.[16] In Indonesia, some of the $2 billion in Japanese aid for the construction of the controversial Asahan Hydroelectric and Aluminum Project has been spent for a nine-hole golf course for employees of the project and Japanese visitors.[17]

Another criticism of tied assistance is that once projects are funded there is little money available for maintenance. The Philippine General Hospital is an example of this problem. Completed in 1989, this hospital contains state-of-the-art equipment acquired from Japan. Unfortunately, parts for repairing equipment must come from Japan and funds are unavailable for these maintenance costs.[18]

There are other more direct costs to recipients which flow from the sectoral concentration of Japanese aid in infrastructure. Infrastructural development carries high potential for detriment both to the environment and to the inhabitants of the recipient countries.

In fact, Japan has been recently criticized for the adverse social and environmental impacts of its aid. A group of environmentalists in both the United States and Japan have begun to compile data on the environmental impact of specific ODA projects. A sampling of these case studies illustrates these concerns.

- In 1982, JICA provided $1.5 million in funds for road construction in a forest area of Sarawak, Malaysia. The road, built through a tropical rain forest, uprooted several indigenous tribes. The tribal inhabitants, concerned that the road and the subsequent logging operations that resulted from the road were destroying their tropical rain forest, fields, and burial grounds, staged a number of protests from 1987 through 1989. The road, however was completed and the indigenous people relocated. As one member of the Berawan tribe stated after being relocated to a government-built village: "We can't adapt to this life, but we have no choice because the jungle has been destroyed."[19]

The logging operations in the tropical rain forests are being conducted by Limbang Trading Limited, a Japanese-Malaysian joint-venture company, which plans to complete the logging of all commercially productive areas in the next ten years.

One observer has commented that "The coincidence of the building of the road and an increase in Japan's imports of tropical timber from Sarawak illustrates how Japan's development funding and Japanese companies can work closely together."[20] In fact, Japan imports more than one-half of the tropical timber cut in the world annually and more than one-half of this total comes from the Sarawak region of Malaysia.[21]

- In 1980, JICA financed several surveys for development of a portion of the Amazon region of Brazil. The Greater Carajas Development Programme is a $62 billion project for "integrated resources development and export processing activities, including promotion of migration into the rain forest and expansion of farmland in the Amazon region of Brazil, over 1,120,000 km. Half of this area is covered by tropical rain forest; it represents 13 percent of the area of Brazil."[22] Japanese financing of the project, which was begun in the mid-1980s, is channeled through both the World Bank and the Export-Import Bank of Japan (EXIM). According to several sources, the project so far has resulted in a significant amount of deforestation of primarily tropical rain forests as well as an uprooting of local inhabitants.

- From 1982 through 1985, OECF, along with the Asian Development Bank and Mitsui, a Japanese bank, financed one-half of the Batang Ai hydroelectric dam in Malaysia. The dam, according to one report, "engulfed 21,000 acres of tropical rain forest in the homeland of 3,000 indigenous Iban people," who were forcibly resettled.[23]
- In Papua, New Guinea, environmentalists claim that Japanese companies are destroying one of the world's last virgin rain forests and diverting profits offshore.[24]

To criticism that their ODA financed projects are more environmentally unsound than other donors, the Japanese government responded by increasing the share of ODA funds for environmental projects and by including environmental impact review in all subsequent ODA projects. There are reasons to conclude that both efforts will be insignificant.

In 1989, Japan announced a $2.2 billion bilateral and multilateral "environmental aid package,"which was intended to increase aid to what the Japanese describe as a new "sector" in development assistance. In an interview with this author, one Japanese official volunteered that it is easy to reclassify ODA projects by sector. In the late 1970s and early 1980s, when most of the major donors began reducing infrastructure-related assistance and emphasizing basic needs and the rural poor, projects that had been classified as infrastructure (like irrigation, waste treatment and water supply projects), were simply reclassified as basic needs or social sector projects. Now, with the current emphasis on the environment, it was this official's informed view that many of these same types of projects will be classified under a new environmental sector. This practice of reclassifying is probably not unique to the Japanese aid program. It was impossible, however, to gather similar information for other donors' programs.

In 1990 both JICA and OECF announced that they would begin to include environmental impact assessments in grant and loan project reviews. Staff limitations in both of these agencies make it unlikely that these initiatives will result in significant changes.

CONCLUSION

Two conclusions flow from the evidence presented in this chapter. First, Japanese aid and trade are linked. Specifically, aid to infrastructure projects in Indonesia, Malaysia, the Philippines, Thailand, China, and Korea is positively correlated with trade in infrastructure. Tied aid benefits the Japanese economy and industries. Capital projects support the exports of Japanese goods.

But do these projects benefit the recipient countries and are they based on their needs? Basic infrastructure is essential for economic growth; and it is clear that the Southeast Asian developing countries—the major recipients of Japanese ODA and of infrastructure related assistance—have witnessed high rates of growth in the last decade. However, the second finding is that many of these same countries are experiencing serious environmental problems that may threaten both growth and human health in the future.

As was already discussed, it is difficult to quantify the precise impact of tied aid on a recipient. Without empirical data on the prices of goods procured using ODA and comparable prices on goods financed without ODA, it is impossible to show direct causal relationships. Nevertheless, there is some evidence that, in general, prices are higher with tied aid, thus reducing the real amount of aid available to the recipient. Moreover, there are other potentially negative results of tied assistance: skewing projects to support the donor's domestic industries reduces a recipient's ability to formulate its own development projects and plans. Moreover, there are potentially serious impacts on the environment and local groups. To fully understand the effects of tied aid on both the donor and recipients, case studies of individual countries and individual projects should be conducted.

Specified Model

$$\text{Trinf} = C + \text{Pop} + \text{GNPCap} + \text{Aidinf}$$

where:

Trinf = Japanese exports in infrastructure to each of the sample countries from 1982–89

C = Constant

Pop = Population

GNP/Cap = Gross national product per capita

Aidinf = Lagged Japanese aid in infrastructure (t-1).

A positive relationship was expected for both the GNP/capita and the aid to infrastructure variables. Countries with higher GNPs, it was hypothesized, have more developed and sophisticated markets and are able to attract more exports. The author posits that aid in infrastructure lays the foundation for subsequent trade in infrastructure.

The results of multiple regression analysis using a straight linear formulation are presented below. Experiments with log-formulations did not fit the data better. Moreover, all relevant assumptions underlying a linear model were tested.

$$\text{TRINF} = -4.908 + .143\,\text{Pop}^* + .03\,\text{GNP/Capita} + .237\,\text{LagAidinf}^*$$

$$R^2 = 82\% \quad \bar{R}^2 = 74\%$$

$$^* = \text{Significant at the .05 level or better}$$

The first statistic one should examine is the adjusted coefficient of determination, or the adjusted $\overline{R}^2$. The adjusted $\overline{R}^2$, which explains the amount of average variation in the dependent variable (trade in exports) attributable to the independent variables (Aidinf, Pop and GNP/Cap), is high at 74% — i.e., for these countries and for these years, that percentage of the variation in exports in infrastructure is explained by the independent variables.

A second important statistic is the t test, which measures the significance of the coefficients associated with the independent variables. In this model, variables that are significant have been starred. Aid in infrastructure is a significant predictor of trade in infrastructure one year later (t statistic greater than 2.0). This means that the relationship between aid in infrastructure and trade in infrastructure is unlikely to be due to random chance. The fact that aid in infrastructure is significant, even with such a small sample, is an important finding. It means, at least for these countries and these years, aid in infrastructure may lay the foundation for trade in a subsequent year.

A multiple regression model relating foreign direct investment, aid in infrastructure, and trade infrastructure could not be built due to insufficient data. A correlation of these variables, however, suggests that Japanese private direct investment is positively (though weakly) related to the aid and trade variables. A full test of these relationships, however, would require additional data.

Correlations with Japanese Foreign investment

Aid in infrastructure	.527
Trade in infrastructure	.312

5

Which Way
the
United States?

IMPLICATIONS FOR
U.S.—JAPANESE RELATIONS

The slow progress of foreign, particularly American, firms to win OECF-financed contracts, underscored by the discrepancy in contract statistics, is likely to aggravate U.S.–Japanese relations. The results on untying do indicate that aid projects funded by OECF are still won almost entirely by Japanese companies. Contrary to what might be expected from statistical information released by the Government of Japan, few foreign companies have actually won OECF-financed contracts.

Japan's loan aid program benefits Japanese business. This is not entirely surprising, but it is, again, contrary to what was expected based on the official data. Any country's aid program is based on a vision of national self-interest. What distinguishes Japan's program from other major donors programs, is: (1) the extent of loans in the overall package, (2) the fact that these loans appear to be de facto tied to Japanese businesses, and (3) their sectoral orientation toward infrastructure. These three factors combine to reinforce the link between aid and Japanese commercial interests.

Such a conclusion could increase the tension between the U.S. and Japan, so it is important also to note Japan's nonproject grant aid program in Africa. While a small portion of Japan's overall ODA program, it is the only example of a foreign aid program that is implemented by independent agencies. Moreover, the findings on Japan's loan program should not blind us to the progress that has been made recently at the government-to-government level on aid policy.

HISTORY OF COLLABORATION

Beginning in the 1960s attempts have been made to coordinate aid policy between Japan and the U.S. Until very recently progress had been stalled. Since the late 1970s at the government-to-government level, some progress has been made in coordinating projects and learning from each others' very different aid programs. Consultations between the administrator of the U.S. Agency for International Development (USAID) and the director general of the Ministry of Foreign Affairs' Economic Cooperation Bureau (ECB) began in 1978 and have been held on an almost annual basis since then. At a more senior political level, then, President Reagan and Prime Minister Nakasone agreed in 1985 that annual meetings between the undersecretary for political affairs and one of Japan's deputy foreign ministers should be regularized. In meetings held in 1989 a significant exchange of views between the two country's aid officials occurred. Moreover, in the same year, AID in conjunction with OECF, JICA, Japan's Ex-Im

Bank, the Ministry of Foreign Affairs and representatives of trading firms held conferences in the U.S. to explain the Japanese aid process to American firms.

While these meetings were useful for learning about one another's aid programs, little has yet been accomplished by both countries in the way of policy coordination. There has been some coordination at the project level, going as far back, surprisingly, as 1969, when the U.S. and Japan jointly financed the Southeast Asia Fisheries Development Program. The U.S. aid documents on this project indicate that the U.S. was involved in this project primarily "to help Japan become more of a leader in development projects in this part of the world."[1] Examples of projects where there has been joint U.S. and Japanese inputs, primarily in technical assistance, are summarized in table 5.1.

More recently, what is called "parallel" coordination, in which parts of a project are handled by separate donors, has emerged as another model of development cooperation between the U.S. and Japan. Parallel coordination has occurred in the past with two projects, in India and in Indonesia. An unusual level of parallel coordination exists in

Table 5.1. U.S. Japanese Aid Coordination: Project Level

Year	Project	Japanese Input	US Input
1969–1971	South East Asia Fisheries Development Center	Fishing vessels, technical assistance; Equipment and Scholarships	$400,000
1979–1984	Indonesia Outer Island Malaria Program	JICA assistance: $560,000 for experts and the services of one entomologist per year, (40,000)	$40 million

Table 5.1. U.S. Japanese Aid Coordination: Project Level, cont.

Year	Project	Japanese Input	US Input
1980	School Education Project in Tonga and W. Samoa	Grant aid $3.5 mil.	Peace Corps
1982	Bataan Refugee Center in the Philippines	Grant aid $7.1 mil.	Financial assistance Peace Corps
1983	Agricultural Development Research Center (ADRC) in Northeast Thailand	Grant aid $8.9 mil.	Financial Assistance Short term experts
1984–1986	Family Planning Project	Equipment and Materials	Financial Assistance Experts
1984–1989	Thailand Provincial Waterworks Authority Institutional Development	JICA Estimated $5.0 million	$5.7 million
1985–1990	Institute of Postgraduate Studies in Agriculture (IPSA) in Bangladesh	Grant aid $13.8 mil. Technical Cooperation	Financial Assistance Experts: Long and short term.
1988	Symposium on Agriculture and Rural Development in Asia	Staff Participation	Sponsor of Symposium
1988–1994	India Quality for Health Technologies	$50 million	$13.3 million

Source: U.S. AID project data base 1960–1991 and Ikufumi Tomomoto, "Some Case Studies on Japan-US Aid Cooperation." Unpublished document.

the recently announced joint U.S.-Japanese infrastructure project in Jamaica and the jointly funded U.S./Japanese/ UNICEF, Mickey Leland Fund.

JAMAICA NORTH COAST DEVELOPMENT PROJECT

On May 1991, the governments of Japan and the U.S. announced agreement on a joint project in Jamaica, the North Coast Development project. The $84 million project, which is designed to rehabilitate essential infrastructure, roads, ports, water supply, and sewage systems, is the first of its kind in Latin American and the Caribbean.

The U.S. agreed to fund the feasibility study and the management costs while the Japanese are funding the bulk of the project. The Japanese have pledged $60 million for the design and construction costs, to be provided on an untied basis. The implementation of the project is to be handled by the Jamaicans, USAID and Japanese officials. It is an interesting example of development cooperation, since it is the first time a major development project has been co-financed by the world's two largest donors.

THE MICKEY LELAND FUND

A program that is much smaller in scope is the Mickey Leland fund. It was established in 1990 in memory of Congressman Mickey Leland, a supporter of humanitarian assistance who was killed in a plane crash in Ethiopia. The project has three major components: direct emergency assistance implemented through UNICEF, and funded ($1 million per year) by the Economic Cooperation Bureau of the Ministry of Foreign Affairs; training for health workers and health professionals from developing countries, funded through the U.S. Agency for International Development (approximately $350,000–400,000 per year); and $100,000 in scholarships for students preparing for careers in development, at Texas Southern University.[2]

Although much smaller in scale than the Jamaican project, this joint initiative to date, has been successful. UNICEF views this project as a "unique opportunity for further AID/UNICEF/ GOJ collaboration."[3] AID, which has a comparative advantage over the Japanese in training for development, also has shown enthusiasm for this project. According to one official, "this is exactly the kind of collaborative venture that we welcome."[4] Finally, the Government of Japan, through this program, has been able to develop desired technical ties with the U.S. development community and enhance its aid image. Project-level and parallel coordination may well continue and even increase in the future, although serious disagreements between the U.S. and Japan over aid policy will probably continue.

IMPLICATIONS FOR THE U.S. FOREIGN AID PROGRAM

One policy outcome from a new assessment of Japanese aid may be a proportionate increase in U.S. funding for capital projects, potentially requiring tied aid financing. When funding for tied aid credits was increased during the late 1980s it was due to a perception that other major OECD donors were using both tied aid and mixed credit programs (a blending of concessional and nonconcessional lending), and a 1989 Eximbank report which concluded that "estimates of capital goods exports lost due to lack of access to markets dominated by tied aid credits range from $400–800 million/year."[5]

As a result of the perception that foreign tied aid has hurt U.S. exporters, several new U.S. programs linking aid and trade have been developed. The U.S. rationale underlying these programs is that the use of tied aid by other donors results in significant trade distortions, and that one way to counter this is to use the U.S. foreign aid program, at least in part, to support U.S. exporters. The U.S. Congress, in the Trade and Development Enhancement Act of 1983, gave authorization to U.S. AID and the Eximbank to jointly provide tied aid credits. The 1988 trade legislation contained in the Omnibus Trade and Competitiveness Act moved authority from this program to a separate institution, TDP or the Trade and Development Program. In addition, a new fund, entitled the War Chest, which was to supplement tied aid credits, was established in 1987 for use by the Eximbank. These funds are targeted toward what are called "spoiled sectors": telecommunications, power, transportation and construction equipment, sectors where tied aid is offered by other countries. Approximately $285 million in War Chest funds has been allocated to these sectors in fifteen developing countries (see appendix 5.1).

It was the original intent of Congress, however, that War Chest funds, as the name implies, would be used as leverage in ongoing discussions with the OECD countries regarding tied aid credits. The U.S. aid posture throughout this period has been to pry others *away* from tying policies.

Agreement on tied aid credits was reached by the OECD countries in November 1991. Called the "Helsinki V" agreement, it "bars OECD members from extending so-called tied aid to the more affluent developing countries such as Singapore, Brazil and Mexico . . . the accord defines such recipient countries as those with a per-capita gross national product of $2,350 a year, or higher,"[6] and prohibits tied aid for commercially viable projects.

Despite this agreement there are strong Congressional pressures today to increase the funding for capital projects, and to tie these funds to U.S. exports. The U.S. Congress is considering legislation that would channel $1.3 billion of U.S. foreign aid over the next two fiscal years into capital projects tied to U.S. exports.

It would be a sad irony if the U.S. effort to promote united aid were to capitulate to the strategy itself. Legislation like that being considered could lead to retaliatory responses from other donors and ultimately hurt the U.S. and the world economy. It is no conjecture that tied aid credit financing, if used by all the major donors, could introduce significant trade distortions in a number of sectors. Moreover, tied aid is very expensive to development. It has been estimated that tied aid credits cost 35 cents per every dollar of exports.

The U.S. should not respond to the Japanese program by reorienting its foreign assistance program toward capital projects without a careful analysis of its past experience in infrastructure- related assistance. Rather, the most instructive lesson offered by a study of this nature is the caveat against building policy on a poor empirical foundation. Indeed, during the 1950s and 1960s the U.S. foreign assistance program was oriented primarily toward infrastructure assistance. While there are very few systematic studies about the U.S. aid experience during this period, a current review of eighty U.S. AID projects in infrastructure illuminates some of the problems inherent in this type of assistance. The projects chosen are the only ones with sufficient evaluative material to include in this analysis.

The projects come from seven infrastructure-related categories: power/electric; construction; roads/highways; integrated development and tourism; telecommunications; irrigation; and potable water and sewage. Fifteen categories of both positive and negative comments were extracted from the evaluation documents themselves. These evaluative comments were categorized and are listed below. Based on this preliminary review, it appears that many of the goals of this infrastructure-related assistance were not met. (A complete list of projects and categories is presented in appendix 5.2.)

For example,
- 17 percent of the projects did not meet their targets or objectives;
- 27 percent were poorly or inadequately managed;
- An additional 34 percent were poorly or inappropriately designed or planned;
- 18 percent had insufficient technical assistance and training;
- 12 percent benefited the target beneficiaries;
- 5 percent were considered to be well-designed;
- Only 6 percent were identified as having improved the physical quality of life of the beneficiaries;
- 9 percent improved public service delivery and or access to it; and
- Only 10 percent increased private sector involvement and a further 12.5 percent spurred other investment.

Finally, from a development perspective, reorienting the U.S. foreign assistance program by linking aid to exports of capital goods would unquestionably hurt the poorer developing countries. Capital assistance goes primarily to the middle and upper income developing countries, many of which could begin to rely on commercial financing. Finally, capital assistance also, as the name implies, is capital intensive and may not take advantage of the relative abundance of labor found in most LDCs, thus limiting any possible employment-generating effects of the assistance.

In conclusion, then, a move by the United States to link aid and trade would be counter to the U.S. historical commitment to free trade. A failure of that commitment at this time could lead to a further unraveling of the international trade regime.

Most arguments for tying U.S. assistance to U.S. exports assume that those exports to the Third World are not increasing and that foreign assistance should be tied to commercial exports. In fact, U.S. exports to the Third World, particularly of capital goods, increased dramatically in the late 1980s.[7] From 1986 to 1990 U.S. merchandise exports to all LDCs increased by 83 percent. This is compared to a 54 percent increase for Japan and 48 percent for the European Community.

What is most striking is that recent and compelling evidence shows that U.S. exports, particularly of capital goods, have increased dramatically to the LDCs that instituted economic policy reforms in the 1980s. These reforms opened up their economies to world trade and reduced domestic distortions. From 1985 to 1989 U.S. exports to countries that instituted policy reform, the "reformers," were twice as great as to the "nonreformers." For example, for the Asian and Latin American reformers, exports increased by 95 percent, compared to approximately 45 percent for countries in these regions which did not institute economic reforms. The figures are similar for the Near East. In Africa, in countries that did not undergo economic reforms, U.S. exports declined by about 10 percent.[8]

Important lessons have been learned from the policy reform efforts of the 1980s, and they are reflected in these statistics. One of the best ways to boost global trade is to ensure that all countries, including those in the Third World, have healthy, growing economies. U.S. foreign assistance, like many other bilateral donors and multilateral agencies in the 1980s, was increasingly focused on encouraging such policy reforms. It would be counterproductive for the United States, for the Third World, and for world trade if aid were once again tied to exports rather than used to encourage broad-based growth and development.

The current era begs for more than tactical approaches by all parties as the U.S. is entering a new relationship with all of its allies, but particularly with Japan. During the Cold War period, fundamental differences in economic policy were subordinate to strategic concerns. Now, economic differences may lead to real conflict, and Japan's bilateral aid policies, unless reoriented, are likely to help fuel that conflict.

Tied Aid War Chest Transactions 1987–1991 (U.S. $ Million)

Country	Project	Export Value	War Chest Grant Amount
FY 1987			
Gabon	Earth Satellite Station	$21.2	$5.3
Gabon	Cellular Telephone System	8.5	2.1
Brazil	Hospital Equipment	35.0	8.7
Brazil	Airport Navigation Equipment	52.6	13.2
India	Gas Turbines	27.0	8.8
Thailand	Capital Equipment	100.0	40.0
	Subtotal 1987	$244.3	$78.1
FY 1988			
Jordan	Power Equipment	18.3	5.5
Algeria	Telecommunications	16.0	2.1
	Subtotal 1988	$34.3	$7.6
FY 1989			
No transactions authorized			

Country	Project	Export Value	War Chest Grant Amount
FY 1990			
China	Shanghai Metro Project	23.2	10.4
Uruguay	Power Project	55.2	19.3
Morocco	Air Traffic Control	24.7	9.9
Philippines	Tied Aid Line	125.0	13.8 *
	Subtotal 1990	$228.1	$53.4
FY 1991			
Indonesia	Tied Aid Line	127.7	56.2
Thailand	Tied Aid Line	127.7	43.7
Pakistan	Tied Aid Line	135.0	—*
Papua New Guinea	Satellite Earth Station	3.1	1.1
Papua New Guinea	Satellite System	13.5	4.7
Indonesia	Telecommunications Equipment	60.0	17.0 *
Mauritius	Construction Equipment	5.0	1.8
Pakistan	Digital Switches	45.0	15.8
Pakistan	Satellite System	15.0	5.2
	Subtotal 1991	$532.0	$145.5
	Total	$1,038.7	$284.5

* $30 million in grants is being provided by A.I.D.
In Pakistan, A.I.D. provided $46 million of grant funds.
In Indonesia, A.I.D. will provide a total of $12 million in grant funds.
Source: Export-Import Bank of the United States, "Semi-Annual Report on Tied Aid Credits," 25 October, 1991, Attachment 2.

Positive and Negative Comments on USAID Infrastructure Projects

Appendix 5.2. Positive Comments on USAID Infrastructure Projects

Project	Proper procure-ment & use of project inputs	Project met or exceeded Targets	Well Managed	Benefitted targeted beneficiaries
Power/Electric				
Egypt Elec Dist (2630001)	x			
India Rural Elec (3860462)		x		x
Bangladesh Rural Elec (3880021)	x	x		
Bangladesh Rural Elec II (3880054)	x	x		
Indonesia Semarang Steam Power (4970204)				
Indonesia West Java Trans Dist I (4970215)		x		
Indonesia West Java Trans Dist II (4970232)		x		
Ecuador Rural Elec Assis (5180099)				
Bolivia Rural Elec II (5110205)		x		
Construction				
Egypt Quattamia Cement (2630052)				
Egypt Urban Low Cost Hlth Delivery (2630065)				
Egypt Low Inc. Hous./Comm. Upgrading (2630066)		x		x

Developed local institutional capacity	Well Designed	Efficient T.A. & Training	Improved Physic Qual. of Life	Costs Kept low
X				
X				
	X			
		X		
		X		
			X	
	X			X

Appendix 5.2. Positive Comments on USAID Infrastructure Projects, cont.

Project	Spurred other invest.	Increased prvt Sector involve.	Improved Public srvc. deliv. &/or access to it	Proper monitoring system used
Power/Electric				
Egypt Elec Dist (2630001)				
India Rural Elec (3860462)				
Bangladesh Rural Elec (3880021)				
Bangladesh Rural Elec II (3880054)				
Indonesia Semarang Steam Power (4970204)				
Indonesia West Java Trans Dist I (4970215)				
Indonesia West Java Trans Dist II (4970232)				
Ecuador Rural Elec Assis (5180099)				
Bolivia Rural Elec II (5110205)				
Construction				
Egypt Quattamia Cement (2630052)				
Egypt Urban Low Cost Hlth Delivery (2630065)				
Egypt Low Inc. Hous./Comm. Upgrading (2630066)				

Community
Participation
increased

Generated
employ-
ment

Appendix 5.2. Positive Comments on USAID Infrastructure Projects, cont.

Project	Proper procurement & use of project inputs	Project met or exceeded Targets	Well Managed	Benefitted targeted beneficiaries
Jordan Vocational Training (2780238)		x		x
Bangladesh Fertilizer Dist Improve. (3880024)				x
Philippines Bicol Intgr hlth. nutr. & pop (4920319)		x		
Guyana Rice Modernization (5040044)	x			
Dominican Rep. Educ Sector Loan (5170119)			x	
Ecuador Primary Educ Improve. (5180027)		x		
Guatemala Small Farmer Mkting (5200238)				
Honduras Ag. Credit & Storage (5220092)				
Paraguay Educ. Dev. (5260095)				
Somalia Rural Hlth Delivery (6490102)				
Kenya Kibwezi Primary Hlth Care (6150179)		x		
Swaziland Coop & Mkting (645055)				
Sudan Primary Hlth Care (650019)				
Congo Smallholder Ag. Dev. (6790001)		x		

Developed local institutional capacity	Well Designed	Efficient T.A. & Training	Improved Physic Qual. of Life	Costs Kept low
		x		
		x		
x	x			
		x		
		x		
x				
		x		
				x

Appendix 5.2. Positive Comments on USAID Infrastructure Projects, cont.

Project	Spurred other invest.	Increased prvt Sector involve.	Improved Public srvc. deliv. &/or access to it	Proper monitoring system used
Jordan Vocational Training (2780238)				
Bangladesh Fertilizer Dist Improve. (3880024)		x		
Philippines Bicol Intgr hlth. nutr. & pop (4920319)	x		x	
Guyana Rice Modernization (5040044)				
Dominican Rep. Educ Sector Loan (5170119)				x
Ecuador Primary Educ Improve. (5180027)				
Guatemala Small Farmer Mkting (5200238)		x		
Honduras Ag. Credit & Storage (5220092)				
Paraguay Educ. Dev. (5260095)				
Somalia Rural Hlth Delivery (6490102)				
Kenya Kibwezi Primary Hlth Care (6150179)				
Swaziland Coop & Mkting (645055)				
Sudan Primary Hlth Care (650019)				
Congo Smallholder Ag. Dev. (6790001)				

Community Participation increased	Generated employment
	x
x	
x	

Appendix 5.2. Positive Comments on USAID Infrastructure Projects, cont.

Project	Proper procurement & use of project inputs	Project met or exceeded Targets	Well Managed	Benefitted targeted beneficiaries
Roads/Highways				
Jordan Yarmouk-Dead Sea Road (2780176)				
Philippines Bicol 2ndary & Feeder Roads (4920281)				
Indonesia Jagorawi Hwy Construc. (4970223)				
Indonesia ACEH Road Betterment (4970241)				
Colombia Small Farmer Mkt Access (5140194)				
Dom. Rep. Rural Roads Main. & Rehab II (5170177)				
Honduras Rural Trails & Access Roads (5220164)		x		x
Malawi Lake Shore Road, Phase I (6120153)	x	x		
Malawi Lake Shore Road, Phase II (6120153)		x		
Kenya Rural Roads Systems (6150168)				
Botswana Transport Sector I (6330073)		x		
Swaziland Rural Reconstruc. (6450224)		x		

Developed local institutional capacity	Well Designed	Efficient T.A. & Training	Improved Physic Qual. of Life	Costs Kept low
x				
x				
		x		
		x		

123

Appendix 5.2. Positive Comments on USAID Infrastructure Projects, cont.

Project	Spurred other invest.	Increased prvt Sector involve.	Improved Public srvc. deliv. &/or access to it	Proper monitoring system used
Roads/Highways				
Jordan Yarmouk-Dead Sea Road (2780176)	x			
Philippines Bicol 2ndary & Feeder Roads (4920281)			x	
Indonesia Jagorawi Hwy Construc. (4970223)				
Indonesia ACEH Road Betterment (4970241)	x			
Colombia Small Farmer Mkt Access (5140194)			x	
Dom. Rep. Rural Roads Main. & Rehab II (5170177)				
Honduras Rural Trails & Access Roads (5220164)	x		x	
Malawi Lake Shore Road, Phase I (6120153)				
Malawi Lake Shore Road, Phase II (6120153)				
Kenya Rural Roads Systems (6150168)				
Botswana Transport Sector I (6330073)				
Swaziland Rural Reconstruc. (6450224)				

Community Participation increased	Generated employ- ment
	x
	x

Appendix 5.2. Positive Comments on USAID Infrastructure Projects, cont.

Project	Proper procurement & use of project inputs	Project met or exceeded Targets	Well Managed	Benefitted targeted beneficiaries
Tunisia Rural Dev Roads (6640305)				
Mali Operations Mils-Mopti Phase II (6880202)				
Integrated Dev./ Tourism				
Jordan Dev Adv Services (2780183)				
Jordan Valley Village Dev II (2780205)		x		
Jordan Village Dev III (2780221)		x		
Sri Lanka Mahaweli Irrig-Water Mgt Rsc. (3830042)				
Philippines Bicol Integr. Dev II (4920310)				
Indonesia Rural Works (4970240)				x
Indonesia Area & Transmigration Dev (4970244)				
Bolivia Disaster Recovery (5110581)		x		
Jamaica Integr. Regional Rural Dev (5320046)				
West Indies Productive Infrastruc. Rehab (5380082)		x		

Developed local institutional capacity	Well Designed	Efficient T.A. & Training	Improved Physic Qual. of Life	Costs Kept low
			X	
			X	
X				
			X	
X				

Appendix 5.2. Positive Comments on USAID Infrastructure Projects, cont.

Project	Spurred other invest.	Increased prvt Sector involve.	Improved Public srvc. deliv. &/or access to it	Proper monitoring system used
Tunisia Rural Dev Roads (6640305)			x	
Mali Operations Mils-Mopti Phase II (6880202)				
Integrated Dev./ Tourism				
Jordan Dev Adv Services (2780183)				
Jordan Valley Village Dev II (2780205)	x	x		
Jordan Village Dev III (2780221)	x	x		
Sri Lanka Mahaweli Irrig-Water Mgt Rsc. (3830042)				
Philippines Bicol Integr. Dev II (4920310)				x
Indonesia Rural Works (4970240)	x			
Indonesia Area & Transmigration Dev (4970244)				
Bolivia Disaster Recovery (5110581)				
Jamaica Integr. Regional Rural Dev (5320046)				
West Indies Productive Infrastruc. Rehab (5380082)				

Community Participation increased	Generated employ-ment
x	
x	

Appendix 5.2. Positive Comments on USAID Infrastructure Projects, cont.

Project	Proper procurement & use of project inputs	Project met or exceeded Targets	Well Managed	Benefitted targeted beneficiaries
Guatemala tourism Infrast. (5960045/01)		x		
El Salvador tourism Infrast. (5960045/02)		x		
Honduras tourism Infrast. (5960045/03)		x		
Nicaragua tourism Infrast. (5960045/04)		x		
Costa Rica tourism Infrast. (5960045/05)		x		
ROCAP tourism Infrast. Feas. Studies (5960045/06)				
Swaziland Coop. & Mkting (6450055)				
Zaire Basic Rural Health (6600086)		x	x	
Ecuador Integr. Rural Hlth. Deliv. System (5180015)				
Jamaica Integr. regional rural Dev. (5320046)				
ROCAP CABEI Integration Fund (5960031)		x		
Telecommunications				
Egypt Telecom Equip (2630054)		x	x	
Eegypt Telecommunications II (2630075)	x	x	x	

Developed local institutional capacity	Well Designed	Efficient T.A. & Training	Improved Physic Qual. of Life	Costs Kept low
		x		
		x		
		x		
		x		
		x		
x				
x				
		x		
x				x
				x

Appendix 5.2. Positive Comments on USAID Infrastructure Projects, cont.

Project	Spurred other invest.	Increased prvt Sector involve.	Improved Public srvc. deliv. &/or access to it	Proper monitoring system used
Guatemala tourism Infrast. (5960045/01)		x		
El Salvador tourism Infrast. (5960045/02)				
Honduras tourism Infrast. (5960045/03)		x		
Nicaragua tourism Infrast. (5960045/04)				
Costa Rica tourism Infrast. (5960045/05)		x		
ROCAP tourism Infrast. Feas. Studies (5960045/06)				
Swaziland Coop. & Mkting (6450055)				
Zaire Basic Rural Health (6600086)				
Ecuador Integr. Rural Hlth. Deliv. System (5180015)				
Jamaica Integr. regional rural Dev. (5320046)				
ROCAP CABEI Integration Fund (5960031)				
Telecommunications				
Egypt Telecom Equip (2630054)				
Eegypt Telecommu- nications II (2630075)				

Community Participation increased	Generated employment
x	
x	

Appendix 5.2. Positive Comments on USAID Infrastructure Projects, cont.

Project	Proper procurement & use of project inputs	Project met or exceeded Targets	Well Managed	Benefitted targeted beneficiaries
Liberia Telecom Expansion (6690111)				
Irrigation				
Egypt Ag. Canal Recons & Maintenance (2630035)		x		
Jordan Sprinkler Irrig. Equip. (2780195)				
Sri Lanka Mahaweli Design & Supervis. (3830056)				
India Rajasthan Med. Irrig. (3860467)				
Philippines Provincial Water (4920263) *				x
Peru Hlth & Environ Sanitation (5270221) *				
Peru Fresh Water Fisheries Dev. (5270144)				
Potable Water/ Sewage				
Egypt Cairo Sewage (2630091)		x		
Jordan Village Dev II (2780221)		x		
Yemen Taiz Water/ Sewerage Contruc. (2790039)				

* Duplicated under Potable Water/Sewage Section

Developed local institutional capacity	Well Designed	Efficient T.A. & Training	Improved Physic Qual. of Life	Costs Kept low
		X		
X		X		
		X		
		X		
			X	

Appendix 5.2. Positive Comments on USAID Infrastructure Projects, cont.

Project	Spurred other invest.	Increased prvt Sector involve.	Improved Public srvc. deliv. &/or access to it	Proper monitoring system used
Liberia Telecom Expansion (6690111)				
Irrigation				
Egypt Ag. Canal Recons & Maintenance (2630035)				
Jordan Sprinkler Irrig. Equip. (2780195)				
Sri Lanka Mahaweli Design & Supervis. (3830056)				
India Rajasthan Med. Irrig. (3860467)				
Philippines Provincial Water (4920263) *	x			
Peru Hlth & Environ Sanitation (5270221) *				
Peru Fresh Water Fisheries Dev. (5270144)				
Potable Water/ Sewage				
Egypt Cairo Sewage (2630091)				
Jordan Village Dev II (2780221)				
Yemen Taiz Water/ Sewerage Contruc. (2790039)	x	x		

* Duplicated under Potable Water/Sewage Section

Community Participation increased	Generated employ- ment
x	
	x
x	

Appendix 5.2. Positive Comments on USAID Infrastructure Projects, cont.

Project	Proper procure-ment & use of project inputs	Project met or exceeded Targets	Well Managed	Benefitted targeted beneficiaries
Philippines Provincial Water (4920263)				x
Indonesia Surakarta Potable Water (4970262)				
Honduras Rural Water and Sanitation (5220166)				x
Peru Hlth & Environ Sanitation (5270221)				
Lesotho Rural Water & Sanitation (6320088)				
Burkina Faso Rural Water Supply (6860228)		x		
Togo Rural Water Supply & Sanitation (6930210)				

Developed local institutional capacity	Well Designed	Efficient T.A. & Training	Improved Physic Qual. of Life	Costs Kept low
x		x		
		x		
x	x			
x				
		x		

Appendix 5.2. Positive Comments on USAID Infrastructure Projects, cont.

Project	Spurred other invest.	Increased prvt Sector involve.	Improved Public srvc. deliv. &/or access to it	Proper monitoring system used
Philippines Provincial Water (4920263)	x			
Indonesia Surakarta Potable Water (4970262)				
Honduras Rural Water and Sanitation (5220166)				
Peru Hlth & Environ Sanitation (5270221)				
Lesotho Rural Water & Sanitation (6320088)			x	
Burkina Faso Rural Water Supply (6860228)			x	
Togo Rural Water Supply & Sanitation (6930210)				

Community Participation increased	Generated employment
	x
x	
x	

Appendix 5.2. Negative Comments on USAID Infrastructure Projects

Project	Improper use of or inavailability of project inputs	Did not meet targets	Poorly or Inadequately Managed	Did not reach targeted beneficiaries
Power/Electric				
Egypt Elec Dist (2630001)				
India Rural Elec (3860462)				
Bangladesh Rural Elec (3880021)			x	
Bangladesh Rural Elec II (3880054)			x	
Indonesia Semarang Steam Power (4970204)			x	
Indonesia West Java Trans Dist I (4970215)				
Indonesia West Java Trans Dist II (4970232)			x	
Ecuador Rural Elec Assis (5180099)				
Bolivia Rural Elec II (5110205)		x	x	
Construction				
Egypt Quattamia Cement (2630052)				
Egypt Urban Low Cost Hlth Delivery (2630065)	x	x	x	
Egypt Low Inc. Hous./Comm. Upgrading (2630066)	x	x		x

Relied on/ Failed to develop efficient local institutions	Poorly or inappropriately Designed or planned	Inefficient T.A. & Training	Experienced serious delays in implementation	High Costs or Lack of financial viability
	x			x
	x	x		x
x	x			x
x				x
	x			
			x	
				x

Appendix 5.2. Negative Comments on USAID Infrastructure Projects, cont.

Project	Personnel Problems (Lack of personnel or high turnover)	Poor co-ordination and commun-ication	Unrealistic timeframe or targets	Lack of proper monitoring system
Power/Electric				
Egypt Elec Dist (2630001)				x
India Rural Elec (3860462)				
Bangladesh Rural Elec (3880021)				
Bangladesh Rural Elec II (3880054)				x
Indonesia Semarang Steam Power (4970204)				
Indonesia West Java Trans Dist I (4970215)				
Indonesia West Java Trans Dist II (4970232)	x			
Ecuador Rural Elec Assis (5180099)				
Bolivia Rural Elec II (5110205)				
Construction				
Egypt Quattamia Cement (2630052)				
Egypt Urban Low Cost Hlth Delivery (2630065)				x
Egypt Low Inc. Hous./Comm. Upgrading (2630066)				x

144

Lack of Community Participation	Untrained or inexperienced staff

Appendix 5.2. Negative Comments on USAID Infrastructure Projects

Project	Improper use of or inavailability of project inputs	Did not meet targets	Poorly or Inade- quately Managed	Did not reach targeted beneficiaries
Jordan Vocational Training (2780238)	x			
Bangladesh Fertilizer Dist Improve. (3880024)				
Philippines Bicol Intgr hlth. nutr. & pop (4920319)				
Guyana Rice Modernization (5040044)				
Dominican Rep. Educ Sector Loan (5170119)		x		
Ecuador Primary Educ Improve. (5180027)				
Guatemala Small Farmer Mkting (5200238)				
Honduras Ag. Credit & Storage (5220092)		x	x	
Paraguay Educ. Dev. (5260095)				
Somalia Rural Hlth Delivery (6490102)		x	x	
Kenya Kibwezi Primary Hlth Care (6150179)				
Swaziland Coop & Mkting (645055)				
Sudan Primary Hlth Care (6500019)	x			
Congo Smallholder Ag. Dev. (6790001)			x	

Relied on/ Failed to develop efficient local institutions	Poorly or inappro- priately Designed or planned	Inefficient T.A. & Training	Experienced serious delays in implemen- tation	High Costs or Lack of financial viability
x				
x				
	x			
		x		x
			x	
		x	x	
x				x
x				
	x	x		

Appendix 5.2. Negative Comments on USAID Infrastructure Projects, cont.

Project	Personnel Problems (Lack of personnel or high turnover)	Poor co-ordination and communication	Unrealistic timeframe or targets	Lack of proper monitoring system
Jordan Vocational Training (2780238)				
Bangladesh Fertilizer Dist Improve. (3880024)			x	
Philippines Bicol Intgr. hlth. nutr. & pop (4920319)		x		x
Guyana Rice Modernization (5040044)				
Dominican Rep. Educ Sector Loan (5170119)	x	x		x
Ecuador Primary Educ Improve. (5180027)	x			
Guatemala Small Farmer Mkting (5200238)				x
Honduras Ag. Credit & Storage (5220092)				
Paraguay Educ. Dev. (5260095)				x
Somalia Rural Hlth Delivery (6490102)				
Kenya Kibwezi Primary Hlth Care (6150179)	x			x
Swaziland Coop & Mkting (645055)			x	
Sudan Primary Hlth Care (6500019)	x			
Congo Smallholder Ag. Dev. (6790001)	x			

Lack of Community Participation	Untrained or inexperienced staff
x	
	x
x	

Appendix 5.2. Negative Comments on USAID Infrastructure Projects

Project	Improper use of or inavailability of project inputs	Did not meet targets	Poorly or Inadequately Managed	Did not reach targeted beneficiaries
Roads/Highways				
Jordan Yarmouk-Dead Sea Road (2780176)				
Philippines Bicol 2ndary & Feeder Roads (4920281)	x		x	
Indonesia Jagorawi Hwy Construc. (4970223)		x		
Indonesia ACEH Road Betterment (4970241)			x	
Colombia Small Farmer Mkt Access (5140194)				
Dom. Rep. Rural Roads Main. & Rehab II (5170177)				
Honduras Rural Trails & Access Roads (5220164)			x	
Malawi Lake Shore Road, Phase I (6120153)	x			
Malawi Lake Shore Road, Phase II (6120153)				
Kenya Rural Roads Systems (6150168)	x			
Botswana Transport Sector I (6330073)	x			
Swaziland Rural Reconstruc. (6450224)				

Relied on/ Failed to develop efficient local institutions	Poorly or inappropriately Designed or planned	Inefficient T.A. & Training	Experienced serious delays in implementation	High Costs or Lack of financial viability
			x	
	x		x	
	x		x	
x				
			x	
		x		

Appendix 5.2. Negative Comments on USAID Infrastructure Projects, cont.

Project	Personnel Problems (Lack of personnel or high turnover)	Poor co-ordination and commun-ication	Unrealistic timeframe or targets	Lack of proper monitoring system
Roads/Highways				
Jordan Yarmouk-Dead Sea Road (2780176)	x	x		
Philippines Bicol 2ndary & Feeder Roads (4920281)				
Indonesia Jagorawi Hwy Construc. (4970223)				
Indonesia ACEH Road Betterment (4970241)	x			
Colombia Small Farmer Mkt Access (5140194)				
Dom. Rep. Rural Roads Main. & Rehab II (5170177)				
Honduras Rural Trails & Access Roads (5220164)	x			
Malawi Lake Shore Road, Phase I (6120153)		x		
Malawi Lake Shore Road, Phase II (6120153)				
Kenya Rural Roads Systems (6150168)			x	
Botswana Transport Sector I (6330073)	x			
Swaziland Rural Reconstruc. (6450224)				

Lack of Community Participation	Untrained or inexperienced staff
	x
x	
	x

Appendix 5.2. Negative Comments on USAID Infrastructure Projects

Project	Improper use of or inavailability of project inputs	Did not meet targets	Poorly or Inadequately Managed	Did not reach targeted beneficiaries
Tunisia Rural Dev Roads (6640305)				
Mali Operations Mils-Mopti Phase II (6880202)	x	x	x	
Integrated Dev./ Tourism				
Jordan Dev Adv Services (2780183)	x			
Jordan Valley Village Dev II (2780205)			x	
Jordan Village Dev III (2780221)			x	
Sri Lanka Mahaweli Irrig-Water Mgt Rsc. (3830042)				
Philippines Bicol Integr. Dev II (4920310)		x		
Indonesia Rural Works (4970240)				
Indonesia Area & Transmigration Dev (4970244)	x		x	
Bolivia Disaster Recovery (5110581)			x	
Jamaica Integr. Regional Rural Dev (5320046)				
West Indies Productive Infrastruc. Rehab (5380082)				

Relied on/ Failed to develop efficient local institutions	Poorly or inappro- priately Designed or planned	Inefficient T.A. & Training	Experienced serious delays in implemen- tation	High Costs or Lack of financial viability
			x	
	x	x		x
			x	
			x	
	x			
x	x	x	x	
	x			
	x		x	x
x				
x				

Appendix 5.2. Negative Comments on USAID Infrastructure Projects, cont.

Project	Personnel Problems (Lack of personnel or high turnover)	Poor co-ordination and commun-ication	Unrealistic timeframe or targets	Lack of proper monitoring system
Tunisia Rural Dev Roads (6640305)	x			
Mali Operations Mils-Mopti Phase II (6880202)				x
Integrated Dev./ Tourism				
Jordan Dev Adv Services (2780183)				
Jordan Valley Village Dev II (2780205)				
Jordan Village Dev III (2780221)				
Sri Lanka Mahaweli Irrig-Water Mgt Rsc. (3830042)				
Philippines Bicol Integr. Dev II (4920310)				
Indonesia Rural Works (4970240)			x	
Indonesia Area & Transmigration Dev (4970244)		x		
Bolivia Disaster Recovery (5110581)				x
Jamaica Integr. Regional Rural Dev (5320046)		x		x
West Indies Productive Infrastruc. Rehab (5380082)			x	

Lack of Community Participation	Untrained or inexperienced staff
	x

Appendix 5.2. Negative Comments on USAID Infrastructure Projects

Project	Improper use of or inavailability of project inputs	Did not meet targets	Poorly or Inadequately Managed	Did not reach targeted beneficiaries
Guatemala tourism Infrast. (5960045/01)				
El Salvador tourism Infrast. (5960045/02)				
Honduras tourism Infrast. (5960045/03)				
Nicaragua tourism Infrast. (5960045/04)				
Costa Rica tourism Infrast. (5960045/05)				
ROCAP tourism Infrast. Feas. Studies (5960045/06)				
Swaziland Coop. & Mkting (6450055)				
Zaire Basic Rural Health (6600086)	x			
Ecuador Integr. Rural Hlth. Deliv. System (5180015)				
Jamaica Integr. regional rural Dev. (5320046)				
ROCAP CABEI Integration Fund (5960031)				
Telecommunications				
Egypt Telecom Equip (2630054)				
Eegypt Telecommunications II (2630075)				
Liberia Telecom Expansion (6690111)				

Relied on/ Failed to develop efficient local institutions	Poorly or inappropriately Designed or planned	Inefficient T.A. & Training	Experienced serious delays in implementation	High Costs or Lack of financial viability
	x	x		
	x		x	
	x		x	
	x		x	
	x		x	
	x		x	
	x		x	
x				
	x		x	
	x			
		x		
		x		

Appendix 5.2. Negative Comments on USAID Infrastructure Projects, cont.

Project	Personnel Problems (Lack of personnel or high turnover)	Poor co-ordination and commun-ication	Unrealistic timeframe or targets	Lack of proper monitoring system
Guatemala tourism Infrast. (5960045/01)				
El Salvador tourism Infrast. (5960045/02)				
Honduras tourism Infrast. (5960045/03)				
Nicaragua tourism Infrast. (5960045/04)				
Costa Rica tourism Infrast. (5960045/05)				
ROCAP tourism Infrast. Feas. Studies (5960045/06)				
Swaziland Coop. & Mkting (6450055)			x	
Zaire Basic Rural Health (6600086)	x			x
Ecuador Integr. Rural Hlth. Deliv. System (5180015)		x		
Jamaica Integr. regional rural Dev. (5320046)				
ROCAP CABEI Integration Fund (5960031)				
Telecommuications				
Egypt Telecom Equip (2630054)				x
Eegypt Telecommu-nications II (2630075)				
Liberia Telecom Expansion (6690111)				

Lack of Community Participation	Untrained or inexpe- rienced staff
x	

Appendix 5.2. Negative Comments on USAID Infrastructure Projects

Project	Improper use of or inavailability of project inputs	Did not meet targets	Poorly or Inadequately Managed	Did not reach targeted beneficiaries
Irrigation				
Egypt Ag. Canal Recons & Maintenance (2630035)				
Jordan Sprinkler Irrig. Equip. (2780195)	x			
Sri Lanka Mahaweli Design & Supervis. (3830056)				
India Rajasthan Med. Irrig. (3860467)		x		
Philippines Provincial Water (4920263) *		x		
Peru Hlth & Environ Sanitation (5270221) *				
Peru Fresh Water Fisheries Dev. (5270144)			x	
Potable Water/ Sewage				
Egypt Cairo Sewage (2630091)	x			
Jordan Village Dev II (2780221)				
Yemen Taiz Water/ Sewerage Contruc. (2790039)	x		x	
Philippines Provincial Water (4920263)		x		

* Duplicated under Potable Water/Sewage Section

Relied on/ Failed to develop efficient local institutions	Poorly or inappro- priately Designed or planned	Inefficient T.A. & Training	Experienced serious delays in implemen- tation	High Costs or Lack of financial viability
	x	x		
			x	
	x	x		
	x			
			x	
	x		x	

Appendix 5.2. Negative Comments on USAID Infrastructure Projects, cont.

Project	Personnel Problems (Lack of personnel or high turnover)	Poor co-ordination and commun-ication	Unrealistic timeframe or targets	Lack of proper monitoring system
Irrigation				
Egypt Ag. Canal Recons & Maintenance (2630035)				x
Jordan Sprinkler Irrig. Equip. (2780195)				
Sri Lanka Mahaweli Design & Supervis. (3830056)	x			
India Rajasthan Med. Irrig. (3860467)	x			
Philippines Provincial Water (4920263) *				
Peru Hlth & Environ Sanitation (5270221) *		x		
Peru Fresh Water Fisheries Dev. (5270144)		x		
Potable Water/ Sewage				
Egypt Cairo Sewage (2630091)				x
Jordan Village Dev II (2780221)				
Yemen Taiz Water/ Sewerage Contruc. (2790039)		x		
Philippines Provincial Water (4920263)				

* Duplicated under Potable Water/Sewage Section

Lack of Community Participation	Untrained or inexperienced staff
	x

Appendix 5.2. Negative Comments on USAID Infrastructure Projects

Project	Improper use of or inavailability of project inputs	Did not meet targets	Poorly or Inadequately Managed	Did not reach targeted beneficiaries
Indonesia Surakarta Potable Water (4970262)				
Honduras Rural Water and Sanitation (5220166)		x	x	
Peru Hlth & Environ Sanitation (5270221)				
Lesotho Rural Water & Sanitation (6320088)				
Burkina Faso Rural Water Supply (6860228)			x	
Togo Rural Water Supply & Sanitation (6930210)				

Relied on/ Failed to develop efficient local institutions	Poorly or inappro- priately Designed or planned	Inefficient T.A. & Training	Experienced serious delays in implemen- tation	High Costs or Lack of financial viability
			X	
	X	X		
				X
		X		
				X

Appendix 5.2. Negative Comments on USAID Infrastructure Projects, cont.

Project	Personnel Problems (Lack of personnel or high turnover)	Poor co-ordination and commun-ication	Unrealistic timeframe or targets	Lack of proper monitoring system
Indonesia Surakarta Potable Water (4970262)			x	
Honduras Rural Water and Sanitation (5220166)				
Peru Hlth & Environ Sanitation (5270221)		x		
Lesotho Rural Water & Sanitation (6320088)	x			
Burkina Faso Rural Water Supply (6860228)		x		
Togo Rural Water Supply & Sanitation (6930210)				

Lack of Community Participation	Untrained or inexperienced staff
	x
x	x

6

Japanese Aid Amidst Global Needs

THE JAPANESE MODEL:
NARROW OR GLOBAL?

In a post–Cold War world, Japan is the largest capital exporter and is likely to shape the debate on aid policy for future decades. The political rationale for the programs of many of the previous major donors has disappeared along with the Cold War, while the U.S. and most European donors now face significant domestic constraints to expanding foreign assistance. In addition, the two major lending institutions set up after World War II to assist the Third World countries, the World Bank and the International Monetary Fund, are beginning to focus their attention on Russia, the newly independent states, and Eastern Europe. This will result in fewer funds being available for the less-developed countries. Thus the Japanese model of development may become the primary model for year to come. What kind of model is it?

The picture of Japanese assistance that emerges from the research presented in this work is a program that is commercially driven. The data establish that the loan component of Japanese official development assistance is effectively tied to purchases from Japan.

The impact of aid in infrastructure financed through loans on Japanese exports in infrastructure is strong and positive. That is, aid financed through loans is positively associated with exports in infrastructure the following year. In short, aid benefits Japanese industry. It is still a narrow, mercantilist model of foreign assistance.

What is the impact of this model on the less-developed countries so far? The majority of Japanese bilateral economic assistance is to Asian developing countries. A preliminary attempt was made to assess the costs of tied aid, but without more empirical evidence it is impossible to assess them in financial terms. It would be important to consider, also, the effect on flexibility—on a country's ability to make the most ideal choices for itself.

Foreign assistance also has much broader impacts: on the environment, on income levels within recipient countries, and ultimately on the recipients themselves. While the Asian recipients have some of the highest growth rates of all the developing countries, all are experiencing pollution and income gaps within their societies. Evidence is emerging that shows that the impact of Japanese aid, particularly on the environment, is very destructive.

What does this model tell us about Japan's role in the world economy? It strongly suggests that Japan does not yet have the type of global vision that helped to reshape the world after World War II. The postwar international economic system was structured around the principles of free trade and open markets.

The Japanese model of development is quite different. The state is much more active and interventionist: business and government work closely together to nurture trade and industrial policies. Japan's aid program reflects this unique brand of capitalism. Called a "capitalist development state" (Johnson 1985), it is a country with: a strong bureaucracy that guides the economy; ruled for decades by one party; and with a close partnership between government and industry.

Bilateral aid policy, except for one program in Africa, is based on mercantilist policies. While in the short run Japanese ODA will benefit the major recipients, it will not, in the long run, contribute to the maintenance of an open world economy. As one Japanese scholar has stated: "the American's belief in a free market and government non-intervention is inconsistent with the Japanese view. From the Japanese perspective, there may exist the 'East Asia model' of economic and social development as an alternative to the American model."[1]

The "East Asia model" of development is likely to lead the world further away from a liberal world order, toward one where managed trade and regional subsystems dominate.

In sum, Japan's foreign aid focus is a narrow one, offering capital projects to areas that are commercially viable and rewarding. While infrastructure is obviously an essential component of economic development, and while Japan's major recipients have enjoyed dramatic growth in their economies over the past decade, the development problems and challenges of the 1990s will require a much broader focus—a focus on human development.

CONCLUSION: DEVELOPMENT ASSISTANCE AFTER THE COLD WAR

The last few years have witnessed unprecedented changes in international relations: In Eastern Europe and the former Soviet Union one of the most influential political and economic ideologies—Marxism—is being replaced slowly by a turn toward democracy, by greater participation in political decision-making, and by free markets. This turn toward a more humane, more broad-based political and economic system is something to celebrate. This is happening not only in Eastern Europe but also in Latin America, where a similar turning away from authoritarian governments toward more democratic governments is occurring. While it is difficult to predict what will happen in the long term in any of these countries, these are encouraging developments for people in these countries and for the rest of world.

Unfortunately, however, many changes in the developing world in the last decade were not so promising. For many countries in Sub-Saharan Africa and Latin America, the 1980s were devastating. Incomes fell and the incidence of poverty increased during this decade.

Three categories of development problems have emerged in the 1990s: those associated with poverty, with growth, and with environmental degradation.

Despite progress in some areas of development, it is estimated that at the end of 1991 that more than one billion people, more than 20 percent of the world's population, are diseased, in poor health, or are malnourished. The greatest problems are in Sub-Saharan Africa where 30 percent of the population is ill and undernourished. The AIDS crisis is devastating Africa, where an estimated 15 percent of the productive population may die by the end of the century. Experts estimate that by the year 2000, deaths from the

AIDS epidemic in Asia, the major recipient of Japanese ODA, may surpass those of Africa.

While some LDCs, particularly the middle-income developing countries, experienced renewed growth in the 1980s, many more have stagnant economies and are still mired in debt.

The debt crisis is still one of the major inhibitors of renewed growth in the developing countries. While some of the Latin American borrowers made progress in renewing growth rates in the 1980s, as a result of domestic policy reforms, the debt crisis has forced many of the developing countries into a corner. Their debts can be repaid only with increased exports. Shrinking global demand and increasing restrictions on their exports will prolong these stagnant growth patterns for both developing and developed countries.

The impact of industrial growth on the global environment is only beginning to be understood. For the first time in history the life-support systems of the planet are being threatened, and many would say destroyed, by human activities. Many serious environmental problems in both the industrialized and Third World must be faced. They include the depletion of the ozone layer, the greenhouse effect, deforestation, and water and land pollution. Evidence that is emerging from Eastern Europe indicates that environmental damage there is devastating.

Japan's support for all of these needs is weak. Its bilateral foreign assistance for basic needs or to what are called the social sectors, defined as education, health and water, and sanitation, while increasing in volume along with overall ODA, peaked in 1984. In that year 14.08 percent of ODA went to this sector; by 1988 that figure had dropped to 9.07 percent.[2]

When total world aid to these sectors is examined, the Japanese share is disproportionately small. From 1984 to 1988 Japanese expenditures in education accounted for only

1.13 percent of total education expenditures; 8.63 percent of expenditures in water and sanitation for rural areas and 17.45 percent for primary health care.[3]

Studies have shown the linkages between economic growth and education. In fact, according to a World Bank study, "increased education of the labour force appears to explain a substantial part of the growth of output in both developed and developing countries since about 1950."[4] Other studies have shown both the direct and indirect relationships between investment in human and physical capital. Research by Jameson and Lau (1982) shows that "investment in improved seeds, irrigation, and fertilizers is more productive, in terms of increased yields, when farmers have four years of primary education rather than none."[5] Wheeler (1980) has shown how improvements in education, health and nutrition lead to increased rates of investment and lower birth rates. The Japanese aid program could make a substantial contribution to Third World development by increasing funding for education and for related social sectors.

In June of 1988, at the Toronto summit, the Japanese government announced a new $30 billion Recycling Plan which was intended to make substantial inroads in solving the debt problem. At least $10 billion of this was made up of previous commitments. It is still unclear how much of this is new money and what part is a component of one of Japan's previously announced plans to "double ODA in five years." It appears that only $3 billion of this is targeted for OECF loans to support economic policy efforts and $6 billion for co-financing projects and structural adjustment loans with the World Bank and other multilateral development banks.

The Japanese response on the environment is also considered insufficient. There is evidence to show the damaging impact of Japan's aid on the environment in several recipient countries. The Japanese response has been to establish a new "sector" for the environment but it is becoming increasingly clear that the environment cannot be treated separately. Considerations of the environment must be integrated into every donors assistance programs, and impact assessments must be made at every step of a development project. Japan's commitment of more than $6 billion at the recent Earth Summit for environmental assistance is a hopeful sign.

The traditionally based perspective underlying foreign assistance addresses the problems of poverty, inadequate health care, and more recently policy reform, debt, and environmental problems. While a political rationale based on security concerns was the core motivating force for many donors of foreign assistance, an economic and humanitarian component was always a part of this accepted, larger perspective on development. Today, with Japan's entry into the field, a broader approach to foreign assistance is giving way to one that is more commercially oriented.

For Japan's bilateral aid program to contribute to development in terms of global exigencies, Japan's priorities need to change:

- Japan's loan program should become "open in structure and effect." The project identification stage needs to become more transparent so that more foreign consultants and producers can become involved in identifying needs at the outset.
- Japan's aid priorities need to be expanded. More should be spent for basic needs and less in the *aid program* for infrastructure.
- Japan needs to work more closely with other industrialized countries to reignite growth in the LDCs and to solve the debt problem. Without a solution, growth will continue to stagnate in the major debtor countries, affecting growth and trade in the world economy.

- Japan needs to broaden her perspective on the environment and conduct impact assessments of each project. Since Japan is lacking experts in natural resource management, specialists from other countries, including the U.S., should be integrated in the aid program.
- Japan's aid program needs to be reorganized and centralized. Legislation defining the mission of foreign assistance should be passed.

Bilateral foreign assistance offers an opportunity for Japan to become a leader, an "engine" in the world economy by providing a public good that would benefit all countries, not just the interests of Japan or a region. In order to accomplish this, foreign aid priorities would need to be reexamined; human development, including assistance for the poorest developing countries, would need to be at least equal to the assistance for the middle-income countries. Japan's loan program needs to become open to all competitive bidders, and Japan needs to work with other donors and develop a workable solution to environmental problems.

Without these changes and without a long-range vision, the Japanese model of development will remain what it is today—essentially one of private foreign assistance. It may become the primary model in the decades to come, but the majority of peoples in the Third World are unlikely to benefit from it.

EPILOGUE

As this book was going to press, the 1991 *OECF Annual Report* appeared, which contained additional information about contractors under OECF loans to foreign government. That information is presented herewith.

Principal Contractors under OECF Loans to Foreign Governments

Country	Date of Approval	Principal Contractors in FY 1990
China	1990.11.28	IHC Holland (Netherlands)
	1986.8.3	Shanghai Machinery Import & Export (China)
India	1988.12.15	Sumitomo Corp./Bharat Heavy Electricals (Japan, India)
	1988.12.15	Pacific Consultants International/Consulting Engineering Services (Japan, India)
	1990.1.12	Mineral Exploration Corporation (India)
	1991.1.12	Mitsui & Co./Bharat Heavy Electrical (Japan, India)
Indonesia	1987.3.18	PT. Kjasa Ubersakti/PT. Genjah Teknik Pratama (Indonesia), Pacific Consultants International/Japan (Indonesia), Transportation Consultants/Japan Electrical/P.T. Jaya C.M. Manggala Pratama (Japan, Indonesia)
	1988.7.5	Japan Railway Technical Service/PT. Metro Transportama Consultant (Japan, Indonesia)

Principal Contractors under OECF Loans to Foreign Governments, cont.

Country	Date of Approval	Principal Contractors in FY 1990
Indonesia, cont.	1988.10.21	PT. Adhi Karya (Indonesia), Nippon Koei/PT. Indah Karya/PT. Paracon Indah Kencana/PT. Dacrea/PT. Arcadia Chandra/PT. Nasuma Putra/PT. Aparc Indonesiua/PT. Perentjana Djaja/PT. Hasfarm Dian Konsultan/PT. Neotama Karya Kencana/PT. Sangkuriang (Japan, Indonesia), Pacific Consultants International/PT. Yodya Karya/PT. Cipta Strada/PT. Deserco Development Services/PT. Delta Tama Waja/PT. Arteri Cipta Rencana/PT. Spektra Adhya Prasarana/PT. Bina Insan Mandiri/PT. Singgar Mulia (Japan, Indonesia)
	1989.12.22	PT. Yala Persada International (Indonesia), Kuk Dong, Const. (Korea), CV. Duta Pertiwi (Indonesia), Pacific Consultants International/PT. Bina Karya/PT. Jasa Mitra Manunggal/PT. Delta Tama Waja Corp./PT. Cipt Strada/PT Multi Phi Beta/PT. Soilens/PT. Firtasari Cendekia Consultant/PT. Yodya Karya/PT. Ateri Cipta Rencana/PT. Fincode International & Associates, INDEC & Associates/PT. Wahana Mitra Amerta (Japan, Indonesia)
	1989.12.22	PT. Nindya Karya/Kumagai Gumi/P.S. Concrete (Japan, Indonesia), Mitsui Engineering & Shipbuilding Co./Mitsui Y Co./Morrison Knudsen Engineers/PT. Decorient Indonesia (Japan, USA, Indonesia), Pacific Consultants International/Japan Electrical Consulting/PT. Inti Fra Cipta (Japan, Indonesia) Kawasaki Steel Corp./Mitsui & Co./PT. Guna Elektro (Japan, Indonesia)
	1989.12.22	Kumagai Gumi/PT. Kadi International (Japan, Indonesia), Kuk Dong Const./PT. Panca Perkasa Inti Konstruksi (Korea, Indonesia) Nikken Consultants/Nippon Koei/PT. Wiratman & Associates/PT. Indah Karya (Japan, Indonesia)
Korea	1987.8.18	Daewoo Corp. (Korea), Ssangyong Construction (Korea)

Principal Contractors under OECF Loans to Foreign Governments, cont.

Country	Date of Approval	Principal Contractors in FY 1990
	1988.6.22	Hyosung Industries (Korea)
Pakistan	1988.11.1	Atlas Cable (Pakistan)
Philippines	1988.1.27	Basic Technology & Management (Philippines)
	1988.1.27	Nippon Koei/TCGI (Japan, Philippines)
	1988.1.27	Nippon Engineering Consultant/DCCD (Japan, Philippines), Pacific Consultants International/Renardet (Japan, Philippines)
	1989.5.26	Katahira & Engineers International/Technics (Japan, Philippines)
	1989.5.26	Pacific Consultants International/Philipp's Technical Consultants (Japan Philippines)
	1989.5.26	Nippon Koei/Sir William Halcrow & Partners/Heuristics Technology and Management Consultants/Certeza Development Corp. (Japan, U.K., Philippines), Pacific Consultants International/Renardet S.A./Urban Integrated Consultants (Japan, Philippines)
	1989.5.26	Katahira & Engineers International/Technics (Japan, Philippines), Nippon Engineering Consultant/CCC (Japan, Philippines)
	1990.2.9	Pacific Consultants International/Renardet (Japan, Philippines)
	1990.2.9	Japan Weather Association/Nippon Koei/ Basic Technology & Management (Japan, Philippines)
Kenya	1989.3.17	SOGEA (France)
Jamaica	1988.11.15	Earle and Associates (Jamaica)
Paraguay	1987.8.26	Pacific Consultants International/Servicio Integral (Japan, Paraguay)
Papua New Guinea	1988.11.25	Pacific Consultants International/Kinhill Kramer PTY (Japan, Papua New Guinea)

183

The U.S. State Department also released information as this book was going to press identifying several U.S. firms which won OECF-financed projects in 1991–92, *years that were not covered in this study.* These companies are: G.E. in Mexico, Peru and Uruguay (1991) for locomotives totaling $40 million; G.E. in the Phillipines (1992) for locomotives, $22 million; Voight-Hydro in China (1992) for turbine units totaling $37 million and Stanley Consultants in Slovenia for a study (1992) costing $1.7 million. Both sets of recent data are encouraging in that they show an increase—perhaps even a trend—in non-Japanese procurement.

NOTES

Preface

1. *The Tokyo Declaration on the U.S.–Japan Global Partnership: Global Partnership Plan of Action (Part I)* United States Department of State, January 9, 1992, p. 2.

1. Toward an Empirical Approach to Important Questions

1. Julia Chang Bloch, "A U.S.-Japan Aid Alliance," in Shafiqul Islam, ed., *Yen for Development.* New York: Council on Foreign Relations Press, 1991, p. 70.

2. Karel van Wolferen, "The Japan Problem Re-Visited," *Foreign Affairs* 69(4) (Fall 1990): 47–48.

3. Ronald Morse, "Japan's Drive to Pre-Eminence," *Foreign Policy* No. 69 (Winter 1987): 13.

4. Ezra F. Vogel, "Pax Nipponica?" *Foreign Affairs* 64 (Spring 1986): 759.

5. Richard Rosecrance and Jennifer Taw, "Japan and the Theory of International Leadership." *World Politics* 62(2) (January 1990): 195–96.

6. Calder, Kent E. "Japanese Foreign Economic Policy Formation: Explaining the Reactive State," *World Politics* 40(4) (July 1988): 518.

7. See Shafiqul Islam, ed. *Yen for Development.*

8. Kazuto Tsuji Ikifumi Tomomoto and Kazumi Goto, "In Search of Closer Collaboration Between Japan and US in the Aid Sphere: A Japanese View." Unpublished paper, Tokyo, 1991, p. 20.

9. Workshop on "Japan as Number One Donor: Japan's Foreign Assistance. Conference on Japan and the United States in Third World Development: Looking to the Future, Missoula, Montana, May 14–19. Unpublished Paper, Introduction.

10. Derek Healey, *Japanese Capital Exports and Asian Economic Development*, Paris OECD, 199, p. 109.

11. Alan Rix, "Japan's Foreign Aid: A Capacity for Leadership?" *Pacific Affairs* 62(4) (Winter 1989/90): 463–64.

12. Robert Orr Jr., *The Emergence of Japan's Foreign Aid Power.* New York: Columbia University Press, 1990, p. 13.

13. Garry D. Brewer and Peter deLeon. *The Foundations of Policy Analysis.* Homewood, Illinois: Dorsey Press, 1978. p. 250.

14. Richard Forrest "Japanese Economic Assistance and the Environment: The Need for Reform." Washington, D.C.: The National Wildlife Federation, 1989, p. 29.

15. Patcharee Thanmai, Japanese and U.S. Aid in Thailand: The Thai Perspective." p. 31. Paper Presented at the Workshop on "Japan as Number One Donor: Japan's Foreign Assistance, Conference on Japan and the United States in Third World Development: Looking to the Future, Missoula, Montana, May 14–19.

16. Richard Forrest, "Japanese Economic Assistance and the Environment," p. 24.

17. Clearly, other industrialized countries "tie" their aid. For example, Canadian, Australian, and European infrastructure-related aid is fully tied to procurement in the donor country. The Japanese however, have published official statistics in the Development Assistance Committee (DAK) and in their annual reports, which show the extent to which their aid program is officially untied. The 1991 *DAC Report* notes the following statistics on tied aid: U.S., 40.2%; France, 40.8%; Germany, 32.5%; United Kingdom, 40.2%; Canada, 36.5%; and Japan, 13.8%.

18. Japan International Cooperation Agency, *Development Study*, Undated.

19. Robert M. Orr Jr., "Collaboration or Conflict? Foreign Aid and U.S.–Japan Relations. *Pacific Affairs.* (Winter 1990): 482.

2. The Structure and Implementation of Japanese Bilateral Assistance

1. According to OECF's *Quarterly Report, Third Quarter, 1991,* twenty-three infrastructure related projects, totaling 129.60 million yen, were approved in October, 1991.

2. See Alan Rix, "Japan's Foreign Aid" and Alan Rix, *Japan's Aid Program: A New Global Agenda.* International Development Issues No. 12 Canberra, Australia: Australian International Development Assistance Bureau, 1990.

3. Robert M. Orr Jr., *The Emergence of Japan's Foreign Aid Power,* p. 18

4. Ministry of Foreign Affairs, *Japan's Bilateral ODA 1990,* p. 23.

5. *Money Japan,* December 1988, pp. 125–126.

6. JICA, *Development Study,* Undated, pp. 14–15.

7. OECF, *Annual Report 1990,* P. 137.

8. Ibid.

3. The Search for Non-Japanese Contractors

1. Ministry of Foreign Affairs, *Japan's Bilateral ODA 1990,* p. 1

2. Phone interview, May 1, 1992, with Don Mickelwait, chief executive officer and founder, Development Alternatives Inc., Bethesda, Md.

3. OECF, Washington office. Facsimile July 10, 1991.

4. Robbins and Myers Company executives claim that they have never bid on OECF projects. AT&T International executives spent several months trying to verify this information and concluded that they had bid on several projects but not won; and Amico Trading Inc., could not be located.

5. According to Robert Muscat, presently a Visiting Scholar at the East Asian Institute at Columbia University and who was acting as an economic advisor to the Thai Government's National Economic and Social Development Board during the time of this project, the Thai-American joint venture company bid against a Japanese company for it. The Japanese and joint venture bids were the same except for the cost of one piece of equipment,

an escalator,which was being supplied by a Japanese firm that gave a lower price to the Japanese company than to the Thai-American company. In Muscat's words, this was "a clear case of discriminatory pricing." (Interview, May 1, 1992.)

6. Jagdish Bhagwati, "The Tying of Aid." in J. N. Bhagwati, and R.S. Eckans, eds., *Foreign Aid.* London: Harmondsworth Publishers, 1970, pp. 238–39.

7. Personal correspondence.

8. Facsimile, Crown Agents, Japan, July 19, 1991.

9. Ibid.

10. Determining the exact home country of a product has become increasingly difficult in the last decade as multinationals from both the industrialized countries and from the developing countries move production to other countries.

11. Facsimile, Crown Agents, Japan, July 19, 1991.

12. Facsimile, Karen Dreher, United Nations Procurement Programme, Office for Project Services, October 9, 1991, and Hideo Suzuki, Ministry for Foreign Affairs, Facsimile, October 2, 1991, "Non-Project Grant Assistance."

13. Facsimile, Crown Agents, Japan July 19, 1991.

4. Tied Aid and Its Outcome for the Donor—and the Recipient

1. Much of the early literature on the "transfer problem" in development economics addressed this issue. See for example, W. J. Ethier, *Modern International Economics.* New York: Norton, 1988.

2. See Catrinus Jepma, *The Tying Of Aid,* Paris: OECD, 1991, Part B.

3. Ibid.

4. In fact, a model relating aid and trade in infrastructure in the same year were negatively related.

5. Jepma, *The Tying Of Aid,* p. 55

6. Ibid., p. 16

7. Ibid., p. 57

8. See J. Bhagwati, "Dependence and Interdependence," In G. Grossman, ed. *Essays in Development Economics.* Oxford: Basil Blackwell Publishers.

9. A study conducted by the Norwegian Ministry of Development Cooperation, reviewed in Jepma, *The Tying Of Aid.*

10. Ibid., Part C.

11. See J. N. Bhagwati, *Amount and Sharing of Aid.* Washington, D.C.: Overseas Development Council, 1970.

12. See Jepma, *The Tying Of Aid.*

13. Ibid., p. 55.

14. Akira Takahashi, "The Impact of Japanese aid on Beneficiaries: Observation in Southeast Asia," p. 8. Paper prepared for the Workshop on Japan as Number One Donor: Japan's Foreign Assistance, Conference on Japan and the United States in Third World Development, Missoula, Montana May 14–19, 1987.

15. See The *Japan Times,* April 7, 1991. p. 7

16. See The *Japan Times,* January 6, 1990, p. 1.

17. "Japan Aid: The Give and Take," *Los Angeles Times,* June 9, 1992, p. A1.

18. See Filologo L. Pante Jr. "Japanese and U.S. Development Assistance to the Philippines: A Philippine Perspective." Paper prepared for the Workshop on Japan as Number One Donor: Japan's Foreign Assistance, Conference on Japan and the United States in Third World Development, Missoula, Montana May 14–19, 1987.

19. *National Geographic* 180(5) (November 1991): 66.

20. Richard Forrest, "Japanese Economic Assistance and the Environment: The Need for Reform." Washington, D.C.: The National Wildlife Federation, 1989, p. 32.

21. *National Geographic.*

22. Forrest, "Japanese Economic Assistance," p. 33.

23. Ibid.

24. "ODA Allegory Promotes Depletion of Rain Forests." The *Japan Times Weekly International Edition,* October 7–13, 1991, p. 3.

5. Which Way the United States?

1. U.S. Agency for International Development, South East Asia Fisheries Development, Project Document, 1969, pp. 15–16.

2. Conversation, with Harold S. Fleming, Senior Programme Funding Officer, Mickey Leland Memorial Fund, UNICEF, 9/19/91.

3. Christian Hougan, "The Mickey Leland Fund: Why it Works." Unpublished memo.

4. Ibid.

5. Export-Import Bank of the United States, "Report to the U.S. Congress on Tied Aid Credit Practices, Washington, D.C. April 1989, p. 221. What was lost in the reviews of the 1989 Eximbank report was a second conclusion which stated: "A cross-check of these micro-findings from a data based macro perspective provides little empirical support of significant harm, to the U.S. economy. While the $400–800 million/year of last sales is reasonable within the context of a normal U.S. market share for capital goods exports to LDC's, the paper cannot find aggregate trends that imply noticeably adverse effects on either U.S. market share or industrial structure." (p. 222).

6. *Wall Street Journal,* November 1, 1991.

7. "American Exports to Poor Countries Are Rapidly Rising." *New York Times* May 10, 1992, pp. 1, 14.

8. Draft Paper on Policy Reform and Growth of U.S. Exports, U.S. AID, 1992.

6. *Japanese Aid Amidst Global Needs*

1. Kazuto Tsuji, Ikufumi Tomomoto and Kazumi Goto, "In Search of Closer Collaboration Between Japan and US in Aid Sphere: A Japanese View." Unpublished paper, February 1990, p. 22

2. OECD, Creditor Reporting System and Chiyo Kanda, "Trends in Bilateral Official Resource Flows to Social Sectors, 1985–1988. August, 1990. Unpublished paper.

3. Ibid.

4. George Psacharopoulos and Maureen Wood Hall, *Education for Development: An Analysis of Investment Choices,* Oxford University Press, 1985 p. 17.

5. Ibid., p. 20.

SELECTED BIBLIOGRAPHY

Angel, Robert C. "Explaining Policy Failure: Japan and the International Economy. *Journal of Public Policy* 18(2) (April-June 1988).

Arase, David. "Japanese Bilateral ODA: Leading Away from Liberalism?" Paper prepared for Presentation at the Joint Annual Convention of the British International Studies Association and the International Studies Association, March 28–April 1, 1989. London.

Bhagwati, Jagdish. "The Tying of Aid." in J. N. Bhagwati and R. S. Eckans, eds., *Foreign Aid*, pp. 235–93. London: Harmondsworth Publishers, 1970.

Bloch, Julia Chang. *A U.S. Japan Aid Alliance: Prospects for Cooperation in an Era of Conflict.* Harvard University Program on U.S. Japan Relations, 1989.

Brewer, Garry D. and Peter deLeon. *The Foundations of Policy Analysis.* Homewood, Illinois: Dorsey Press, 1978.

Brooks, William L. and Robert M. Orr Jr. "Japan's Foreign Economic Assistance." *Asian Survey* 25(3) (March 1985):322–340.

Calder, Kent E. "Japanese Foreign Economic Policy Formation: Explaining the Reactive State," *World Politics* 40(4) (July 1988): 517–41.

Caldwell, Alexander. "The Evolution of Japanese Economic Assistance Cooperation, 1950–1970." In Harold B. Malmgren, ed. *Pacific Basin Development: The American Interests,* pp. 61–80. Lexington, Massachusetts: Lexington Books, 1972.

Clifford, Juliet. "The Tying of Aid and the Problem of 'Local Costs.' " *Journal of Development Studies* 2 (1965): 153–73.

Coverdale, A. G. and J. M. Healey, "The Real Resource Costs of Untying Bilateral Aid." *Oxford Bulletin of Economics and Statistics* 43 (1981): 185–199.

Cronin, Richard. *Japan, the United States and Prospects for the Asia-Pacific Century: Three Scenarios for the Future.* Forthcoming: Institute of Southeast Asian Studies.

—————— "Japan's Expanding Role in the Asia-Pacific Region: Alternative Scenarios." *Business and the Contemporary World* (Winter 1992): 111–116.

Ensign, Margee M. "A Review of Japanese Foreign Assistance," House Foreign Affairs Committee, Congressional Research Service, 1985.

Export-Import Bank of the United States. "Report to the Congress on Tied Aid Credit Practices," Washington D.C., April 1989.

Forrest, Richard. "Japanese Economic Assistance and the Environment: The Need for Reform." Washington, D.C.: The National Wildlife Federation, 1989.

Frankel, Jeffrey. "Is A Yen Bloc Forming in Pacific Asia? *Finance and the International Economy: AMEX Bank Review* (1991): 5–20.

Goto, Kazumi. "Japan's Growing Role in International Development and Future Prospects of Japan-US Aid Collaboration in an Era of International Interdependence." Unpublished Paper, Tokyo, 1991.

Healey, Derek. *Japanese Capital Exports and Asian Economic Development.* Paris: OECD, 1991.

Hewitt, Adrian. "Japanese Aid: More than a Rising Sun." *Multinational Business* (Winter 1989): 18–27.

Inoguchi, Takashi. "Four Scenarios for the Future." International Affairs (Winter 1988–89): 20–23.

Inoguchi, Takashi and Daniel I. Okimoto, eds. *The Political Economy of Japan, Volume 2, The Changing International Context.* Stanford: Stanford University Press, 1988.

Islam, Shafiqul, ed. *Yen for Development: Japanese Foreign Aid and the Politics of Burden-Sharing.* New York: Council on Foreign Relations Press, 1991

Jameson, David T. and Laurence J. Lau. *Farmer Education and Farmer Efficiency.* Baltimore: Johns Hopkins University Press, 1982.

Japan International Cooperation Agency. Annual Reports.

Japan, Ministry of Foreign Affairs, Japan's Official Development Assistance Annual Reports (In English and Japanese).

Japan Economic Institute. *Japan's Foreign Aid Policy: 1990 Update* Washington, D.C., 1990.

"Japan's Foreign Aid Program Fuels Asia's Economic Boom." *Journal of Commerce,* April 22, 1992.

"Japanese Businessmen, Government Collaborate on Foreign Aid Contracts." *Journal of Commerce* April 23, 1992

Jepma, Catrinus. "The Impact of Untying on the European Community Countries." World Development 16(7) (1988): 779–805.

——— *The Tying of Aid* Paris: The Development Center of the Organization for Economic Cooperation and Development, 1991.

Johnson, Chalmers. "Political Institutions and Economic Performance: The Government-Business Relationship in Japan, South Korea, and Taiwan." In Robert Scalapino, et. al., eds. *Asian Economic Development: Present and Future.* Berkeley: Institute for East Asian Studies, 1985.

——— MITI and the Japanese Miracle: The Growth of Industrial Policy, 1925–75. Stanford: Stanford University press, 1982.

Jun, Nishikawa. "Japan's Economic Cooperation: New Visions Wanted." *Japan Quarterly* (October–December 1989): 392–403.

Koppel, Bruce and Michael Plummer. "Japan's Ascendancy as a Foreign Aid Power." *Asian Survey* 29(11) (November 1989): 1043–56.

Kubota, Akira. "Foreign Aid: Giving With One Hand?" *Japan Quarterly* 22(2) (April–June 1985).

Moon, Chung-in. "Conclusion: A Dissenting View on the Pacific Future." In Stephan Haggard and Chung-in Moon eds. *Pacific Dynamics: The International Politics of Industrial Change.* Boulder, Colorado: Westview Press, 1989.

Morse, Ronald. Japan's Drive to Pre-Eminence. *Foreign Policy* No. 69 (Winter 1987): 3–21.

Nowels, Larry Q. "Foreign Aid Policy Issues: Japan's Global Role." Congressional Research Service, 1990.

———— "Japan's Emergence as a Leading Foreign Aid Donor." *CRS Review* (July 1989): 14–16.

Orr, Robert M. Jr. "The Aid Factor in U.S.–Japan Relations." Vol. No. *Asian Survey* (July 1988).

———— *The Emergence of Japan's Foreign Aid Power.* New York: Columbia University Press, 1990.

———— "Collaboration or Conflict? Foreign Aid and U.S.-Japan Relations." *Pacific Affairs* (Winter 1990): 476–88.

Overseas Development Council. "An Increased Japanese Role in Third World Development." *Policy Focus* No. 6 (1988):1–11.

Pharr, Susan J. "Japan's Foreign Aid: Testimony Before the House Foreign Affairs Committee, Subcommittee on Asian and Pacific Affairs, September 28, 1988.

Preeg, E. H. "Trade, Aid and Capital Projects." *The Washington Quarterly* (Winter 1989): 173–185.

———— "Japan's Development Aid." *Institutional Investor* (September 1991): 18–19.

———— *The Tied Aid Credit Issue: U.S. Export Competitiveness in Developing Countries.* Washington, D.C. The Center for Strategic and International Studies, 1989.

Pressman, Jeffrey and Aaron Wildavsky. *Implementation.* Berkeley: University of California Press, 1979.

Psacharopoulos, George and Maureen Woodhall. *Education for Development: An Analysis of Investment Choices.* New York: Oxford University Press, 1985.

Rix, Alan. "Japan's Aid to Indonesia: The Case of Mitsugoro." *Pacific Affairs* 52(1) (Spring 1979): 42–63.

—— *Japan's Economic Aid: Policy Making and Politics.* London: Croom Helm, 1980.

—— "Japan's Foreign Aid: A Capacity for Leadership?" *Pacific Affairs* 62(4) (Winter 1989/90).

—— *Japan's Aid Program: A New Global Agenda.* International Development Issues No. 12 Canberra, Australia: Australian International Development Assistance Bureau, 1990.

Rosecrance, Richard and Jennifer Taw. "Japan and the Theory of International Leadership." *World Politics* 62(2) (January 1990): 184–209.

Rowley, Anthony. "Donor's Dilemma." *Far Eastern Economic Review* 10 October 1991.

Stokes, Bruce. "Japan's Asian Edge." *National Journal* (6/29/91): 1620–1625.

Thanmai, Patcharee. "Japanese and U.S. Aid in Thailand: The Thai Perspective." Paper Presented at the Workshop on "Japan as Number One Donor: Japan's Foreign Assistance, Conference on Japan and the United States in Third World Development: Looking to the Future, Missoula, Montana, May 14–19.

—— *The Tokyo Declaration on the U.S.-Japan Global Partnership: Global Partnership Plan of Action (Parts I and II)* United States Department of State, January 9, 1992.

Tsuji, Kazuto, Ikifumi Tomomoto, and Kazumi Goto, "In Search of Closer Collaboration Between Japan and US in the Aid Sphere: A Japanese View." Unpublished paper, Tokyo, 1991.

Tomomoto, Ikufumi. "Some Case Studies on Japan-US Cooperation." Unpublished Paper, Tokyo, 1991.

Van Wolferen, Karel. *The Enigma of Japanese Power.* New York: Knopf, 1989.

Vogel, Ezra F. "Pax Nipponica?" *Foreign Affairs* 64 (Spring 1986): 752–67.

Waterhouse, Brian. "Japanese Giants Roll Across Asia." *Asian Business* 25(10) (October 1989): 64–67.

Wheeler, D. *Human Resource Development and Economic Growth In Developing Countries: A Simultaneous Model.*

World Bank Staff Working Paper, No. 407, Washington, D.C. 1980.

Yasutomo, Dennis T. *The Manner of Giving: Strategic Aid and Japanese Foreign Policy.* Lexington, Massachusetts: Lexington Books, 1986.

―――― "Why Aid: Japan as an Aid Great Power." *Pacific Affairs* 62(4) (Winter 1989/90).

INDEX